MICHAEL WIESE PRODUCTIONS
www.mwp.com

Since 1981, Michael Wiese Productions has been dedicated to providing novice and seasoned filmmakers with vital information on all aspects of filmmaking and videomaking. We have published more than 50 books, used in over 500 film schools worldwide.

Our authors are successful industry professionals — they believe that the more knowledge and experience they share with others, the more high-quality films will be made. That's why they spend countless hours writing about the hard stuff: budgeting, financing, directing, marketing, and distribution. Many of our authors, including myself, are often invited to conduct filmmaking seminars around the world.

We truly hope that our publications, seminars, and consulting services will empower you to create enduring films that will last for generations to come.

We're here to help. Let us hear from you.

Sincerely,

Michael Wiese
Publisher, Filmmaker

"Action-Adventure screenwriting must be every bit as much about character, story, and drama, as it is about action and violence — which is why Neill's book is so important, and will soon become the bible for all genre screenwriters."

—Christopher Wehner
author, *Screenwriting on the Internet*;
founder, The Screenwriters Utopia
(www.screenwritersutopia.com)

"Hicks' new book isn't a 'how-to' book, it's a 'why-to' book. He not only presents the case that Action-Adventure films can be intelligent and well crafted, but backs it with solid information and examples. Anyone with an interest in Action-Adventure, good writing, and good film, will enjoy this book."

—Sable Jak
Scr(i)pt Magazine

"*Writing the Action-Adventure Film* is a challenging, intelligent book that dares to approach screenwriting as a valid form of literary and cultural expression. In all, Hicks has packed a wide-ranging exploration of the historical and cultural underpinnings of Action-Adventure into a slim volume that examines why Action-Adventure is the single most popular, enduring, and exportable genre."

—Daphne Charette
writer, *The Sword and the Rose*;
president, The Screenplayers
(www.screenplayers.net)

"Once this book is read and digested by the Hollywood pros and the wannabes, I expect to see some terrific Action-Adventure films in the theatres. Neill Hicks is a real pro. He is inspiring. He knows the subject. And he demystifies the process."

—Donie Nelson
Career Strategies for Writers

"Dreaming about writing the next *The Matrix*, *Gladiator*, *The One*, or *Spy Game*? Neill clearly knows the Action-Adventure genre inside and out. I recommend the book highly!"

—Eric Lilleør
Publisher/Editor-In-Chief
Screentalk Magazine
(www.screentalk.org)

WRITING THE
ACTION-ADVENTURE
FILM

THE MOMENT OF TRUTH

BY

NEILL D. HICKS

Published by Michael Wiese Productions
11288 Ventura Blvd., Suite 821
Studio City, CA 91604
tel. (818) 379-8799
fax (818) 986-3408
mw@mwp.com
www.mwp.com

Cover Design: Art Hotel
Book layout: Gina Mansfield

Printed by McNaughton & Gunn, Inc., Saline, Michigan
Manufactured in the United States of America

©2002 Neill D. Hicks

Library of Congress Cataloging-in-Publication Data

Hicks, Neill D., 1946–
    Writing the action-adventure film: the moment of truth/
    by Neill D. Hicks.
      p. cm.
    ISBN 0-941188-39-6
    1. Motion picture authorship. 2. Adventure films. I. Title
    PN1996.H49 2001
    808.2'3--dc21

                                                    2001046784
                                                          CIP

TABLE OF CONTENTS

ACTION-ADVENTURE — A SCREENWRITER'S MEDIUM

BY
CHRISTOPHER WEHNER
Editor, *ScreenwritersUtopia.com*

Action-Adventure films are this country's greatest export when it comes to movies. God help us, it is often these films by which many other cultures get their first glimpse of American culture and values. Since you're someone who is interested in writing in this genre, you'll want to know what makes for a complete, satisfying, and worthy Action-Adventure story, and you'll want to avoid some of the problems that afflict most action stories today.

Good Action-Adventure writing is not simply about CGI effects, pyrotechnics, and gratuitous violence. It's about the creation of a complete story that leaves your audience feeling satisfied, and not cheated. It's about substance, not just style.

When we examine together the best the genre has to offer, you might be surprised to learn that Action-Adventure storytelling is defined by more than just intensity. A movie of this genre can offer many different levels of dramatic and thematic style, and the corresponding expectations of moviegoers will influence how you go about writing a script of substance.

Too often screenwriters fail to get the audience emotionally and morally aligned. Shouldn't we care about the protagonist? We as an audience must allow ourselves to enter the world the writer has created on the page.

I first encountered Neill's writing in 1995 when I read an essay of his entitled, "The Underlying Morality of Action-Adventure Films" in an issue of *Creative Screenwriting*, an essay that must have been the impetus for this book. He writes:

> Whether or not movies may be reflecting a new *fin de siècle* morality, the fact remains that to send an audience out of the theater satisfied they have seen a complete story which somehow makes sense out of the experience of change, the screenwriter must establish the structure of a belief system for the characters.

Neill goes on in the article to tell us that as screenwriters we must always be concerned with the "overall meaning of the story, not [just] in the immediate titillation of individual scenes." Too often aspiring screenwriters miss the forest for the trees. While concentrating on the action sequences, the development of a dramatically appealing story habitually gets lost. As with any form of screenwriting the Action-Adventure screenwriter has to render a story. There are moments of truth and realization in our lives as human beings, and so it shall be with our characters. The audience must feel the pain, sorrow, and regret of our Action-Adventure heroes. Our story's protagonists can have faults, just like us. They can be vulnerable to their own

Kryptonite, and still survive by the skin of their teeth. That's what makes them so appealing.

In Jeb Stuart and Stephen E. de Souza's *Die Hard*, we as an audience fear for John McClane's life because there is a building full of bad guys trying to kill him. But most importantly we are connected to him, and sympathize with him. In one of the most important scenes in the movie, McClane is in the bathroom, beaten-up and bloodied, and the situation is not looking good for him. But in this moment of weakness he radios Officer Powell in the squad car outside the building to tell his wife that he is sorry for not being a very good husband: "She was the best thing that ever happened to a bum like me." If you look closely at *Die Hard*, you will see it's really a love story about a guy trying to get back together with his wife.

Action-Adventure screenwriting must be every bit as much about character, story and drama, as it is about action and violence — which is why Neill's book is so important, and will soon become the bible for all genre screenwriters.

CHAPTER 1

WHY TO

There are no magical formulas in this book. Even a 19th-century patent medicine huckster would blush at the extravagance of the claims made by all the proponents of the so-called revolutionary, ten-easy-steps to pain-free screenwriting manuals that are currently on the market. This book is, instead, the first in a series of contemplations on the elusive aspects of screenwriting that have been largely ignored by the fill-in-the-blanks systems. It is not so much a how-to book as it is a *why-to* book.

The international success of *Screenwriting 101: The Essential Craft Of Feature Film Writing* among film executives as well as screenwriters has confirmed the need for a framework of operational definitions — within an industry where promotional exaggeration often determines a film's financial worth rather than the actual cinematic product itself.

> **15 MINUTES** – Action and Comedy rated R for strong violence, language, and sexuality. A police detective investigates a brutal murder committed by a psychopath in this driving action-suspense thriller.

Evaluation by hype is nowhere more evident than during the weeks preceding the voting for the Academy Awards.

Production companies spend vast amounts of money promoting their films, not only through the use of massive advertising in the industry trade papers *Hollywood Reporter* and *Variety*, but also with the distribution of elaborate press kits to the voting members of the Academy. It is the purpose of these Hollywood Happy Meals to secure good "buzz" for the film, whether or not the members ever actually watch the movie. Of course, the publicity departments of studios do much the same thing on a larger scale, hoping to create a fashion of "must-see" public awareness that predisposes an audience to like a film through collective fervor. Studios have even been criticized for creating phony critics' quotations in advertising blurbs, and as many as ten class-action lawsuits have been filed alleging that the public was duped by favorable movie reviews from critics lavishly entertained by the studios.

Conversely, it seems there is no end to the proliferation of self-anointed film reviewers in the alternative press and in public broadcasting who are so impatient to turn their backs on Hollywood films that they have suckered themselves into a latter-day version of the 1960s director-as-auteur personality cult. But, because they lack any solid theoretical construct on which to base an insightful analysis, they can offer only hyper-puffed pop-babble to vindicate their favorite out-of-industry directors and actors.

Adding to the dilemma, the film departments in some of the nation's universities and colleges have concentrated on teaching visual skills as dominant over verbal, while almost completely neglecting the cinematic history that is the *literature* of the medium. As a consequence, few film students graduate with more than an "I like it. It has a good beat..." elementary critical capacity by which to evaluate the movies they see, and they have only the most meager acquaintance with the body of distinguished cinematic work that came before they ever touched a camera or a keyboard.

The *Screenwriting 101* genre books, therefore, are intended to ease some of the ill-conceived judgments that are hastily handed down on scripts, the mistaken labels applied to movies by studios and reviewers alike, and the ornamental ballyhoo that bamboozles not only the public, but screenwriters themselves. It is the goal of these books to provide a set of tools to quarry our way out of the sludge so that all the members of the filmmaking team can collaborate on a more *audience-focused* motion picture experience.

Naturally, there is a built-in liability when theorizing about any creative endeavor, because hypothetical assumptions can easily be mistaken as rigid instructions. The genre books *are not* intended in any sense to provide a *formula* for writing. Writing is far too full of magic and wonder to be reduced to a predictable procedure. Besides, any foolproof formula for screenwriting implies that there is a simultaneous blueprint for exactly how a movie audience reacts. No matter how earnestly many screenwriters, producers, studio executives, financiers, and theater owners would love to have such a magic recipe, there simply ain't no such thing.

Just because there is no unfailing blueprint, however, does not mean that there is no excellence in screenwriting. Screenplays themselves are elaborate puzzles. They may seem to be born whole from a writer's intuition, but the real work of writing is to burrow and jab and poke into that great Gordian knot of an idea until its intricacies have been exposed and the writer deciphers the hidden rules that somehow hold the enigma together. Professional screenwriting is not an uninhibited emotional scrawl. It is a disciplined outpouring of the soul, where the writer keeps constant watch over the concealed veins and mortised junctions that turn the puzzle into a flawless array of imagery rousing the spirit of the audience.

"THIS WRITING BUSINESS. PENCILS AND WHATNOT. OVERRATED IF YOU ASK ME."

— *WINNIE-THE-POOH*, A. A. MILNE

Please read this book with a pencil in your hand.

If you already have an idea for an Action-Adventure film, this is a good place to doodle notes in the margins. If you don't have an idea right now, that's okay too. The **Scribble Exercises** appear throughout the book to help ground the theoretical information in day-to-day-level experience and bring out a spontaneous reaction that may develop into an Action-Adventure premise.

In any event, keep in mind that you do not have to give birth to a perfect screenplay all at once. Writing is a process, not a product. Your imagination is a great block of marble that you will continue to chip away at until the work becomes a beautiful sculpture.

If you disagree with this book, by all means, argue. Make notes. Fight. Come up with your own explanations — but keep on reading.

Once you've finished this book, you will never again accept the description "Action-Adventure" at face value.

Chapter 2

The Expectations of Genre

Time is what keeps everything from happening all at once. Space is what keeps everything from happening to you.

From the Latin *genus* through the Old French for *kind*, English has taken the word *genre* to mean a category of artistic composition marked by a distinctive style, form, or content. In the past, the term was frequently used in a limited scope to describe films such as "B" Horror movies, Saturday morning serials, or the *film noir* Detective films of the 1940s. More recently, the sense of the word has expanded beyond the limits of second-tier movies to include, in one form or another, all films, so that we can now speak of an action-suspense-romance-comedy genre. Of course, this kind of linguistic hodgepodge results because there are no universally agreed upon guidelines to distinguish one genre from another. Yet, through experience as much as anything, the audience has developed an anticipation for the context elements which it expects a particular genre to satisfy. It is up to the screenwriter to provide a **Cosmos of Credibility**, a **Narrative Trajectory**, a **Bounded World**, a **Plausible Moment**, and a **Character Ethos** that all allow the audience to give up its vigilant fix on everyday reality, and willingly to suspend an innate wariness of the unreal. In this way, even though there may not be *rules* as such, it is possible to quantify senses of meaning that distinguish one genre from another.

The diagram at the end of this chapter is the **Genre Continuum**, first introduced in *Screenwriting 101: The Essential Craft Of Feature Film Writing*. The investigation of subatomic physics has taught us that frenzied matter smidgens never really exist in a fixed place, but only have a *tendency* to be there. As soon as we look where we think they are, they're gone. The analysis of genre storytelling is equally frustrating because for nearly every example that seems to illustrate a genre, we can probably find a dozen very similar films that don't agree. However, like a physicist's cyclotron, the Genre Continuum can provide a useful stop-motion image of a genre's constituent parts captured long enough for investigation.

The Genre Continuum is not intended to be an industrial jig for stamping out identical products, so there are no steel walls separating the compartments. Imagine instead that it is a supple, stretchy template where the cells are bounded by semi-permeable membranes. Some elements can migrate through the walls from one genre to another. The continuum may not be one-hundred-percent foolproof for any particular film; but on the whole, it can help identify the elements that writers and producers need to pin down in order to gauge how well their stories do or do not fulfill certain audience expectations.

Because there are no universally accepted definitions of genre, there is also no common agreement on exactly what films or types of films constitute a genre. Are love stories a genre because they contain relationships between men and women? Well, there are many films that are "love" stories that are not about the relationships between men and women at all, nor are they gay-themed films. *Rain Man* is, in fact, a love story between two brothers. Is science fiction a genre? That depends on how the definition is applied. *Star Wars*, *Alien*, *Aliens*, and even *Sixth Sense* might all be said to be science fiction because of their locales or their divergence from our everyday reality, yet there are very basic differences among the films. *Alien* fills all the requirements on the Genre Continuum as a Thriller, while *Aliens* and *Star Wars* are clearly Action-Adventure stories. The Genre Continuum attempts to sort films by their underlying elements rather than by their immediately observable surface characteristics. Naturally, a genre may share some elements of its personality with nearby neighbors, or even with its distant relatives, but if there is a benefit to the examining of genres at all, then we must find some relatively irreducible conditions that form boundaries around each type of film.

WHAT YOU *DON'T* SEE IS ALWAYS WHAT YOU GET.

THE GENRE CONTINUUM

✓ **PRIVATE ANGUISH** — Many European films; early Ingmar Bergman films.

❏ **Narrative Trajectory** — These stories tend to be about characters' self-revelation through the expiation of guilt or imagined guilt. There is very little narrative plot because the events are contained largely inside the character. The Narrative Trajectory, then, is as unfixed as the main character, having no clear end point that the audience can foresee.

❏ **Bounded World** — Because the stories are essentially static, they occur in enclosed, usually small places that physically entrap the main character in internal anguish.

❏ **Plausible Moment** — The time line is fairly short, but follows the intense climax of a lifetime of distress.

❏ **Character Ethos** — The characters are existential, tormented by their own self-doubts.

✓ **PIVOTAL CONFLICT** — *Ordinary People*; *Terms of Endearment*; *Tender Mercies*; *Steel Magnolias*; *Marvin's Room*.

❑ **Narrative Trajectory** — Generally, estranged family members are forced into interpersonal conflict at an emotionally sensitive event such as a funeral, which sets the scene for reviving and resolving old wounds.

❑ **Bounded World** — The action occurs in a box-like, inescapable setting that forces the characters to deal with their quarrels. These films of Pivotal Conflict in characters' lives are often made from material that originally appeared as stage dramas occurring in one room or primarily in one room.

❑ **Plausible Moment** — The intensity of the Pivotal Conflict usually occurs over a short period of time such as a weekend or a couple of days because the sheer intensity of the emotions demands that the characters resolve their discord relatively quickly.

❑ **Character Ethos** — These characters are perhaps the most frail, vulnerable, dimensional, and thoroughly *human* in movies because their conflicts are the most like those experienced by ordinary audience members.

✓ **COMEDIC DRAMA** — *Modern Times*; *The General*; *Bringing Up Baby*; *La Cage aux Folles*; *Tootsie*; *As Good as it Gets*.

❑ **Narrative Trajectory** — Comedic Dramas are about adults acting like children. There is a basic misunderstanding, a leap to the wrong conclusion that is never dealt with rationally. The characters are intimidated by a fascinating and bewildering world they are unprepared to deal with.

❑ **Bounded World** — The comedy world is a giant banana peel, intimidating, exaggerated, and filled with slick things and precarious people.

❑ **Plausible Moment** — Because of the exaggeration of the story, the audience recognizes that the unreality of comedy cannot exist forever; thus time is intense, frenetic, and short.

❑ **Character Ethos** — Comedy characters are the most nihilistic in cinema. They can get away with virtually anything within the riotous world defined by the film, but are generally still held accountable by the audience for the morality of their actions.

✓ **FAIRY TALE** — *Pretty Woman*; *The Piano*; *Sense and Sensibility*; *Good Will Hunting*; *Titanic*.

❑ **Narrative Trajectory** — Fairy Tale characters must release themselves from the emotional bondage that they are subjected to by more dominant characters, who are customarily family members

❑ **Bounded World** — The physical world is as restrictive as the main character's emotional or spiritual world, e.g., a sinking ship, a rural hamlet, or a primitive island.

❑ **Plausible Moment** — Time is most often controlled by the characters themselves as they choose whether or not to act on their own behalf.

❑ **Character Ethos** — Characters are emblematic rather than dimensional, and very sharply defined as good or bad.

✓ **PERSONAL QUEST** — *Quiz Show*; *Chariots of Fire*; *Dead Man Walking*; *The Shawshank Redemption.*

❑ **Narrative Trajectory** — The main character is compelled to define and achieve a personal quality, such as integrity or honesty, because of a moral crisis that demands immediate action.

❑ **Bounded World** — The Personal Quest often occurs in a physically constrained situation such as a prison or hospital, or a position that is outside of the main character's control, such as the military, a sports team, or a corporation.

❑ **Plausible Moment** — It may take weeks or months for the main character to come to grips with the Personal Quest, although an extreme event will always loom as the consummate trial for the main character's integrity.

❑ **Character Ethos** — These characters struggle with the conflict between an equivocal virtue versus moral certitude to determine the value of integrity.

✓ **DETECTIVE** — *Chinatown*; *The Maltese Falcon*; *The Usual Suspects*; *Se7en*; *Silence of the Lambs*.

- ❑ **Narrative Trajectory** — On the backside of civilization, the detective tries to restore equilibrium to a society that has developed a malignant infection.

- ❑ **Bounded World** — The detective, with or without badge, patrols a decaying world of shadows and urban detritus.

- ❑ **Plausible Moment** — Time is blurred, neither day nor night, and as vaporously shrouded as an intoxicated stupor.

- ❑ **Character Ethos** — The detective is a thinker, a character of wits rather than physical strength, who seeks the truth even on the shady side of the street.

✓ **HORROR** — *Frankenstein*; *Dracula*; *Friday the 13th*; *Halloween*; *Poltergeist*; *Invasion of the Body Snatchers*.

❏ **Narrative Trajectory** — A supernatural monster has absolute power over its human victims, who must discover its secret vulnerability in order to survive.

❏ **Bounded World** — Horror exists in a distorted world riddled with secret passageways and unknown recesses, isolated from any outside salvation.

❏ **Plausible Moment** — Because isolation is essential, the intense action occurs over a very short time, usually twenty-four hours or less.

❏ **Character Ethos** — The characters are *everyman*, extremely vulnerable, yet resourceful, representing the best of the human spirit engaged in a battle against the evil of an inhuman fiend.

✓ **THRILLER** — *Three Days of the Condor; North by Northwest; Alien; Breakdown; Single White Female.*

❑ **Narrative Trajectory** — The audience explores its own fears by experiencing an intense emotional identification with the main character's willingness to stay alive.

❑ **Bounded World** — The main character is trapped, isolated from help in an expressionistic extension of our internal fears of abandonment.

❑ **Plausible Moment** — The extreme isolation from outside help requires a very short, but intense time line to remain credible.

❑ **Character Ethos** — A relatively naive character is drawn into a larger and larger intrigue, and discovers that the only way to remain alive is through self-reliance, by exposing the malevolent evil before it can assault the larger community.

✓ **ACTION-ADVENTURE** — All Westerns; war movies; cops and robbers films; *Braveheart*; *Star Wars*; *Independence Day*; *The Guns Of Navarone*; *Con Air*; *Saving Private Ryan*.

❏ **Narrative Trajectory** —The main character knowingly undertakes an impossible mission to save a society from a state of siege, and willingly faces death to defend a personal code of honor that the society shares as a value.

❏ **Bounded World** — The surroundings are open, available for action, and beyond everyday experience.

❏ **Plausible Moment** — Often a sense of weeks, months or even years during which a state of siege builds unbearable tension th   ɪust be broken by decisive action.

❏ **Character Ethos** — Characters who are willing to die for an idea, code, society, or value battle equally motivated antagonists who are *morally different* in a showdown moment of truth.

✓ **METAPHYSICAL DEFIANCE** — *Crimes and Misdemeanors; Amadeus.*

❑ **Narrative Trajectory** — The main character risks an immortal soul by challenging the authority of a self-indulgent Almighty.

❑ **Bounded world** — A sophisticated setting, usually surrounded by the trappings of power and position, where characters have achieved the status of gods on earth.

❑ **Plausible Moment** — The main character only slowly comes to recognize that the struggle is against God.

❑ **Character Ethos** — Characters are intelligent, highly successful, but morally untested, and battle to exert their self-concept over that of an irrational, unjust God.

A WELL-TOLD LIE IS WORTH A THOUSAND FACTS.

The distinctive characters and themes that play out in these various genres have become, over time, the story context elements that the audience looks for in order to trust that the stories they watch will end with emotional satisfaction — and, maybe even spiritual or intellectual enlightenment. In other words, we watch what we enjoy — and we expect to enjoy what we watch.

19

Of course, no one wants to see the same movie or the same kind of movie all the time. However, if you enjoy detective stories, then there are certain elements you are going to look forward to seeing in a detective film, and other things you definitely do not expect to happen. You will be immensely disappointed if, out of nowhere, an NYPD detective decides to abandon the murder case he's working on, marry a circus clown, and move to Brazil, or if the psychopathic murderer turns out to be an enraged canary.

This example may be ridiculous, but more often than we'd like, movies manage to mistakenly incorporate fatal flaws in their structure because they do not pay sufficient attention to the underlying genre conventions.

In *Copycat*, for instance, Sigourney Weaver is a psychiatrist who studies serial killers, but who suffers from agoraphobia and is terrified to set foot beyond her door. As you might expect, a serial killer begins to threaten her through her only link to the outside, her computer. So far, this premise has the making of a good Thriller, not unlike *Wait Until Dark*, where Audrey Hepburn is a blind woman menaced inside her apartment. However, rather than maintaining the tight confines of a Thriller, the film breaks the contract by adding Holly Hunter as a cop hot on the trail of the killer. Now the audience is uncertain of just what kind of movie they're supposed to be watching. Is this a Thriller with Sigourney Weaver in jeopardy, or is this an Action-Adventure with Holly Hunter as a trained, armed, dedicated police officer in pursuit of a killer? These are two acutely dissimilar lead characters (not to mention competing movie stars) forced to function in conflicting story contexts. The consequence is that we literally do not know what to care about.

In another rupture of the genre context, the story for *Last Action Hero* confuses the issues of reality vs. fantasy so thoroughly that the audience is numbed trying to figure out what kind of picture they're watching. A young boy, Danny, is given a "magic ticket" to a new film starring his hero, Arnold Schwarzenegger's Jack Slater. The magic ticket transports Danny from the "real" world into the fantasyland of the movie which, to his amazement and our bewilderment, is populated by "real" good guys and bad guys just like on the movie screen. One of the nastiest bad guys, Benedict, manages to get hold of Danny's magic ticket and skip out of movieville to run amok on the streets of Danny's "real" world in the movie we in the audience are watching. Now, Jack Slater and Danny must stop Benedict before he can kill the "real" actor who plays the fantasy character Jack Slater. Is this film an Action-Adventure? Well, it has all the Schwarzenegger gymnastics you would expect, but the plot logic has so thoroughly invalidated any good sense the audience has of time and place, it becomes a mishmash of action sequences that have absolutely no discernible purpose.

Conceptually, it is not impossible to have movie characters stepping off the screen to interact with the real world. In fact, Woody Allen does just that in work as close to cinematic genius as you can get, *The Purple Rose Of Cairo*. The inherent flaw in *Last Action Hero* comes from ignoring the expectations of the genre, or more to the point, not abiding by the rules of any specific genre. Because the audience members are located neither in the world of reality nor in the world of fantasy, they do not perceive any threat to their own well-being via the danger to the main character. By the time Benedict crashes into the world of the film that the audience is watching, in the context that should be "real," it is far too late to feel any menace.

Last Action Hero offers us double-facing mirrors: the unreality of the movie we are watching placed in front of the unreality of the movie-within-the-movie we are watching. Lost in the infinite reflections of those mirrors, pretty soon there's no anchor point to define where we are. The disorientation of narrative place is the worst thing that can happen to an audience.

Another example: An experienced older cop and a quick-thinking young rookie are on the trail of a sadistic serial killer. So far, this premise could apply to any number of movies from the detective genre, from *Silence of the Lambs* to any variation on the *Lethal Weapon* Action-Adventure franchise. That is precisely the problem with *The Bone Collector*. Denzel Washington's quadriplegic homicide detective Lincoln Rhyme may be giving the orders, but he is literally incapable of carrying them out, so, like Sigourney Weaver in *Copycat*, his imprisoned character is much better suited as the protagonist for a Thriller. On the other hand, his assistant, Angelina Jolie, must carry out all the movements of an Action-Adventure main character. To make matters more confused, the finale of the story rebounds into Thriller mode as the killer appears out of the blue from Rhyme's past, in spite of almost no reference to Rhyme's past in the Action-Adventure story, leaving the audience frantically bewildered about who the hell is doing what to whom and why. This kind of interior-exterior byplay between the minds and actions of the characters is a frequent device used successfully in novels, where the reader has omniscient access to their inner thoughts and feelings on the page. But that gateway is simply not available to movie audiences. Thus, both faithful renditions of books and careless identification of functional story elements can often result in disappointing screen material.

"FIRST LEARN TO DO WHAT YOU WANT. THEN YOU CAN DO WHAT YOU LIKE."

— ZEN PROVERB

In addition to providing ways to classify films, the Genre Continuum also ranks the genres in a specific sequence from left to right, starting with films of Private Anguish where characters are trapped within themselves, and ending with those rare films of **Metaphysical Defiance** where mankind directly challenges God. The order of the progression is derived from the challenge faced by the main character, how that main character ultimately acts to resolve the challenge, and how that action not only changes the society contained in the context of film, but, by extension, how the character's actions connect the movie audience to that changed society.

The first section of the Genre Continuum contains films in the **Private Anguish**, **Pivotal Conflict**, **Comedic Drama**, **Fairy Tale**, and **Personal Quest** genres, all of which share a fundamental goal: the main character seeks to make life more complete, to live a richer existence in some fashion. For example, one of the most popular film genres is the Fairy Tale. In fact, the most commercially successful film of all time, *Titanic*, owes its phenomenal achievement in part to the fact that the sequential this-happens-and-because-of-it-that-happens plot is easy to grasp. All of the characters are clearly good or bad. In spite of the momentous tragic event which constitutes the context for *Titanic*, the doomed love affair of a young man and woman is universally identifiable, and our identification with this story gives the ill-fated love affairs of our own past a kind of majesty that makes sense. This elegant simplicity, along with other elements, is shared by *Pretty Woman*, *Good Will Hunting*, *Moulin Rouge*, and dozens of other successful films that, for the purposes of genre classification here, are Fairy Tales.

All of these films have certain structure, character, and context elements that are nearly identical. However, although there may be a film about two people in love on a doomed ship, without all of the other Fairy Tale elements, it would not necessarily fall into the Fairy Tale genre. *The African Queen*, for instance, is about two people on a doomed boat who fall in love, but the film is decidedly an Action-Adventure story rather than a Fairy Tale. The defining difference is what influences the actions of the lovers Jack and Rose in *Titanic* wield on their fates, their immediate society, and the society of the audience. Of course they influence Rose's fiancé and her mother, but these people are about to be greatly overwhelmed by events outside of Rose's power. The remaining fact is that the love affair between Jack and Rose does not change the surrounding society one bit. Nothing they do has any effect whatsoever on the social order, world affairs, or on who does what to whom in any larger sphere. So, although the emotion of the story can, and obviously does, have an enormously potent impact on the audience, that audience is not bound to any societal change caused by the actions of the main characters. Furthermore, the risks that the main characters take are comparatively small. The principal goal for the two lovers in *Titanic* is to improve their individual lives, that is, to enlarge their joy and become fully alive. The risks these characters take, although they may be emotionally terrifying, do not have lethal consequences. Failure to achieve the goal of happily-ever-after may lead to despondency, but nobody expects to risk death in the process. In *Titanic*, although Jack does indeed die, he does not anticipate that possibility anymore than the others on the ship, and, in fact, his death is not actually compelled by the plot.

The middle section of the Genre Continuum includes the **Detective**, **Horror**, and **Thriller** genres. Although all of these genres share some common elements, and all of them both borrow and lend elements to Action-Adventure, they are distinct forms involving different characters who seek different goals. The overriding trait they have in common is that the main characters in each are ultimately faced with making a choice about their willingness to stay alive. When the chips are down, when the character is all alone and there is no help available, will that character reach inside to find the strength required to remain biologically functional? It would be a great liberation for the character of Ripley in *Alien*, for instance, to simply give up and let the monster chow down, especially when she finds herself locked in the escape pod with the rapacious beast. Why not just roll over and call it a bad day? Because, aside from the fact that the audience would howl in protest, such a surrender would absolutely violate the expectations of the Thriller genre. These are stories about ordinary people unprepared for their circumstances who are pushed to the extreme, cornered, and tormented until they consciously decide to pull the trigger in order to save their own lives.

It is in the final division of the Genre Continuum that **Action-Adventure** resides — unique in the demands it makes of the main character, incredibly powerful in the emotions it inspires in the audience, and by far the most eclectic in context. War movies, Westerns, cops and robbers, some sports stories, historical epics, disaster films, and some science-fiction and fantasy films are all included in the great stew pot of Action-Adventure. Furthermore, sample the ragout and you'll find similar plots with entirely different flavors. Both *The African Queen* and *Romancing the Stone* are romances where two unlikely lovers thrown together by fate are astonished to find themselves in love with their opposites. *Titanic* is also a romance where two unlikely lovers are thrown together by fate. But *Titanic*, as we have seen, is a romance built on a Fairy Tale structure while *The African Queen* and *Romancing the Stone* are both Action-Adventure films.

If not for the pressure of World War I and Rosie's patriotic commitment to sail the *Queen* down the river and blow up the German gunboat, Charlie Allnut and Rosie would never, ever get together long enough to fall in love. Without the overriding Action-Adventure plot, the love story of *The African Queen* simply would not happen. Likewise, Joan Wilder and the American adventurer Jack Colton in *Romancing the Stone* would just sit and glare at each other if there were no treasure map and no *el corazón* emerald at stake. It is the Narrative Trajectory of Action-Adventure that makes the romance possible. Even though these are love stories slung under Action-Adventure plots, each of these two films obviously has a very different ambiance from the other. *Romancing the Stone* is a comedy with a rakish touch of unreality, while the actions in *The African Queen* are much more grounded in reality.

If the Action-Adventure genre can embrace so many different types of stories that also contain so many different variations in mood and texture, how can such a hodgepodge be usefully defined? The answer lies not in the events shown on the screen, but in the core values that buttress the genre like the caissons holding up a bridge.

THE GENRE CONTINUUM

⬆ INCREASING PERSONAL JEOPARDY EQUALS ⬆ INCREASING SOCIETAL CONSEQUENCE

WILLINGNESS TO BECOME FULLY ALIVE					WILLINGNESS TO LIVE			WILLINGNESS TO DIE	
PRIVATE ANGUISH	PIVOTAL CONFLICT	COMEDIC DRAMA	FAIRY TALE	PERSONAL QUEST	DETECTIVE	HORROR	THRILLER	ACTION-ADVENTURE	METAPHYSICAL DEFIANCE
Many European films; early Ingmar Bergman films.	Ordinary People; Terms of Endearment; Tender Mercies; Marvin's Room; etc.	Modern Times; The General; Bringing Up Baby; Tootsie; As Good as it Gets; etc.	Pretty Woman; The Piano; Good Will Hunting; Titanic; Moulin Rouge; etc.	Dead Man Walking; Quiz Show; Shawshank Redemption; etc.	Se7en; The Maltese Falcon; Chinatown; Usual Suspects; Silence of the Lambs; etc.	Poltergeist; Frankenstein; Dracula; Friday the 13th; Halloween; etc.	North by Northwest; Three Days of the Condor; Alien; Breakdown; etc.	Braveheart; Gladiator; Star Wars; Guns of Navarone; Saving Private Ryan; etc.	Crimes and Misdemeanors; Amadeus; etc.

CHAPTER 3

THE FUNDAMENTAL ACTION-ADVENTURE FILM

MOVIES AND MANIFEST DESTINY

Action-Adventure films are consistently the most popular export of American movies, capable of drawing enormous audiences worldwide across many differing societies, ethnicities, and languages. Yet, while overseas audiences flock to see Americans in American Action-Adventure films, when foreign-produced Action-Adventure films attempt to employ the same canon of underlying values — disregard for propriety, disdain for authority, and, above all, independent action — the local films are often regarded as implausible within their own societies.

A case in point is an American script for a Scandinavian co-production about a young law graduate who is posted to the far north country of the Lapps as a kind of circuit justice of the peace and sole local representative of the national law. The young man is immediately confronted with the sometimes-violent conflict between the rights of the indigenous Lapps, and a pipeline company's destruction of reindeer migration corridors. By training, the unseasoned young marshal insists on dealing out the law letter by letter, as the book dictates, but his approach is totally inadequate for the ruthless aggressiveness of the pipeline company as well as the unnerving evaporation and abrupt reappearance of the Lapps. When murder enters the mix, the hero is forced to stop hiding behind detached paper statutes, and must take the authority of the practical law into his own hands in order to keep the land from erupting in an uncontrollable slaughter.

As an American Action-Adventure, this basic story might take place in any number of places with only slight changes in time and character. It could, for instance, occur on an American Indian reservation in the early 1900s, or deep in a South American jungle, or on the remote frontier of some desert. The actual particulars are more or less interchangeable. For the Scandinavians, however, the story is thoroughly unbelievable, even preposterous. They are culturally unable to identify with a character who autonomously takes control and acts independently to rectify a situation. Although they readily accept and enjoy an American character doing exactly the same thing in the context of an American setting, it is beyond credibility to them that a Scandinavian character would commit such an outrageous action within their own culture.

Many of the animated Walt Disney features, from *Pocahontas* to *The Lion King*, although not, strictly speaking, Action-Adventure, are not very far removed from the genre. It is axiomatic that Walt Disney movies, with their superb technical animation, the very special Disneyesque characters, and even a unique overlay of humor are regarded as sure-fire hits, and universal crowd pleasers throughout the world — except in India. The films of Walt Disney, which are so embedded in the cultural consciousness of Americans, have virtually no attraction whatsoever throughout most of the Indian sub-continent.

The American brand of *gimme-an-ax-and-a-gun-and-git-the-hell-outa-my-way* individualism is hardly a familiar personality trait across the pond, either. For the most part, our British forbears have limited their home-grown Action-Adventure films to the covert and derring-do exploits of WWII specialist heroes. In films such as *The Man Who Never Was*, the British put a premium on stealth and the intellectual outwitting of the enemy rather than head-on confrontation. Of course, during World War II, at least, the feisty island had little opportunity to act any other way, so their version of Action-Adventure films celebrate that indomitable spirit. Even the inheritor of that tradition, the immensely popular James Bond franchise, is firmly fixed in the cloak-and-dagger persona.

Other European filmmakers have generally found it equally awkward to make American-style Action-Adventure films about their own cultures because the values required simply do not seem plausible to a European mindset. By the time the Mediterranean shrug of resignation migrates past the impudent Gallic snort to Scandinavia, the Norwegians and Danes actually have a "law" called the *Jante-loven* to protect themselves from making risky decisions. The *Jante-loven* is originally a satiric fictional law drawn from literature. Nevertheless, it has become a very real and powerful cultural edict in Scandinavia that declares, "You shall not think you are smarter than the rest of us, and you shall not risk any action that might be regarded as morally unfit." The result of this deeply-seated value is that decisions, sometimes even the most uncomplicated ones, are nearly always avoided in favor of someone higher up the social/political scale.

In all fairness, the circumspect view of the world that seems to be so engrained in the European mentality is a direct result of the little guy being bent over the barrel by wars, governments, the Church, class structure, and ethnic/religious pecking orders so repeatedly for hundreds of years that the individual has very little sense of any power over destiny. It is not unexpected, therefore, that European cinema rarely conjures up a spirited tale of a little David walloping a giant Goliath.

Nevertheless, there are certainly some non-American films that give the surface impression of being Action-Adventure movies. However, even a passing examination of these claimants reveals that they are founded in cultural and narrative conventions that are wholly dissimilar to the mythology that drives the bona fide romp-and-stomp American Action-Adventure tale.

"I Am That I Am"[1]

The first European films that come to mind as mock Action-Adventure movies are the *spaghetti westerns* produced by director Sergio Leone in the 1960s and 1970s. These mannered art collages of American Western paraphernalia vaulted Clint Eastwood, a barely known TV and "B" movie actor, to international superstardom due to his flinty-eyed, clenched-jaw portrayal of "the man with no name." Indeed, like the Bible's Old Testament God, Eastwood's anonymous deity materializes from the heavens; he doth strike the wicked dead with his terrible

---

[1] Exodus 3:14.

swift six-shooter, and vanishes as tight-lipped as he arrives. Eastwood's resolute malice, though, is far from the amoral character that some have described. He is, instead, a hirsute, vengeful deity come to visit terrible retribution on the confounded entanglements of mankind, and thus to bring the world to order. These spaghetti western films are essentially very Catholic tableaus of the stability imposed on a pagan Europe by the might of the Church.

"YOU ALWAYS USE VIOLENCE. I SHOULD'VE ORDERED GLUTINOUS RICE CHICKEN."

— TYPICAL HONG KONG FILM DIALOGUE SUBTITLES

In Hong Kong, the Chinese have developed a movie industry based almost exclusively on endless repetitions of martial arts postures. The undisputed superstars of these Asian chop-'n-flop exhibitions are Bruce Lee and Jackie Chan. Each man carefully has constructed a special cinematic persona for himself in the social order of the Hong Kong film industry, and ultimately each has secured the devotion of fans in more than half the world's population. It is not at all farfetched to say that, in much of Asia at least, the two men are revered as gods. Their actions are worshiped and their very dialogue is often taken as undisputed truth.

But for all the excitement, grace, and skill of slam-bang action in Hong Kong films, the narrative structure of these movies has adopted nothing from Western Action-Adventure storytelling. The underlying motivations for Hong Kong action films are derived from classic Chinese literature such as *Outlaws of the Marsh*, the fourteenth-century novel which provides ethical instruction via a loosely connected series of individual tales about the adventures of a collection of kind-hearted outlaws who fight for the people against a corrupt government.

In much the same way, the choreographed tango of stylized violence in Hong Kong action films is suffused with straightforward moral parables of right and wrong. Jackie Chan defeats the bad guys in a dazzling tour de force of hands and feet. His opponents, stunned by what is indisputably his superior spiritual power, yield to his moral preeminence, instantly renounce their evil ways, and become on-the-spot converts to the force of good. Their problem is not that they have been bad, but that they have been corrupted by some evil force into abandoning the essential good of their natures. Now that they have been smacked again with the fundamental truth of virtue, they are freed from the beguilement. However, in the nature of parables, no character in this scenario is ever actually accountable for his own behavior. Enlightenment exists *a priori* and need not be wrenched from the individual's guts, but requires only an intermittent booster vaccine delivered by someone on a higher spiritual plane.

Of course, the fact that hundreds of such films do not fit an American Action-Adventure model does not suggest that any of these movies — from the early Russian historical extravaganzas of Eisenstein and Pudovkin to the exquisite Samurai fables of Akira Kurosawa — are in any sense lesser films. Nevertheless, the mere fact that these films contain *action*, does not in itself qualify them as included in the Action-Adventure genre that this book investigates.

Likewise, other film genres — from the Thriller to the Pivotal Conflict — may make liberal use of certain Action-Adventure tools, but hot pursuits, hot lead, and hot-headed slugfests do not, by themselves, make a satisfying Action-Adventure film. To cadge from the neighbor's storeroom does not give the borrower an actual claim on the title to the land. Moreover, there comes a time when overindulgent borrowing turns larcenous; at that point, not only is the integrity of the genre violated, but so is the trust of the audience.

THE FOUNDATION OF ACTION-ADVENTURE FILM

✔ **A STATE OF SIEGE** where the hero battles against over-whelming opposition to achieve an Impossible Mission and save a threatened society from extinction.

✔ **A ROMANTIC EXPLOIT** that transports us to a world removed from our daily existence, where the stakes are life and death, and the characters act with an intensity and nobility that we would possess if only we could.

✔ **A STATEMENT OF MORAL PRINCIPLE** where characters who live by a code of right and wrong are willing to die for their values in a Showdown for truth against formidable enemies made of *morally different* substance.

CHAPTER FOUR

THE GENESIS OF THE ACTION-ADVENTURE FILM

THE ONE WHO TELLS THE STORIES RULES THE WORLD.

— HOPI PROVERB

The storytellers of a civilization are the curators of the myths that order the chaos of everyday life into manageable, understandable sequences of events. Whether gathered around the communal fire pit or seated in a darkened theater, society collects to hear the myth-maker impart stability to experience, and, over the course of these allegorical yarns, to reaffirm the values, attitudes, beliefs, history, champions, assets, and institutions that make up our culture.

Recently, there has been a great deal of talk in the movie industry about the analysis of film stories from the perspective of myth, particularly with regard to Chris Vogler's valuable study of the work of Joseph Campbell. In *The Writer's Journey*, Vogler distinguishes a twelve-stage journey for the hero in all stories:

1. The hero is introduced in his ordinary, mundane world, where the audience discovers his ambitions and limitations, and forms a bond of identification.

2. The hero is challenged by a call to adventure to undertake a quest or solve a problem.

3. The hero is reluctant, and balks at the threshold of adventure because of the fear of facing the unknown.

4. The hero meets a wise mentor, a counselor who encourages the journey.

5. The hero commits to the journey, and crosses over the threshold into a Special World.

6. The hero gathers allies in the Special World, but also encounters challenges and enemies.

7. The hero prepares himself for the coming confrontation with the forces of defeat.

8. The hero endures the supreme ordeal and faces the possibility of death.

9. The hero is reborn by facing death, and discovers new strength.

10. The hero travels out of the Special World to return to the ordinary, but is pursued by the vengeful forces from whom he has captured a treasure.

11. The hero faces the ultimate test on the verge of returning home.

12. The hero returns to the ordinary world with the treasure, and shares his knowledge for the benefit of the community.[2]

---

[2] *The Writer's Journey: Mythic Structure for Writers*, 2nd Edition, by Christopher Vogler. Studio City: Michael Wiese Productions, 1998.

A screenwriter may find this breakdown of story steps very useful in many circumstances when trying to analyze the structural balance of certain kinds of narratives. In fact, the next chapter will examine a comparable set of building blocks used to craft the *audience-focused sequence* that creates a story structure intended to evoke an emotional response from the audience.

Star Wars has often been held up as the clearest example of Campbell's observations applied to movie storytelling. Indeed, if you trace Luke Skywalker's path through the film with Vogler's map in your hand, you can clearly see the parallels. There are, however, a couple of not-so-obvious snags with the Vogler/Campbell model when it comes to examining Action-Adventure films.

In the first instance, what Campbell called the mono-myth — those units of the overarching human chronicle that have been repeated for all mankind throughout all cultures for all time — concentrates on the arrangement of detached particulars in a cross-cultural narrative. This version of the *every-culture* allegory tends to make it at least seem as if all stories follow exactly the same pattern. Consequently, analysts who have tried to squeeze various films into the Campbell model have discovered that to do so requires some rather fancy hammering and carving. For the purposes of Action-Adventure, however, we need to look not so much at the step-by-step structural outline, but at the values recounted in a particular body of mythic tales that impact the spirit of a particular society.

Another inconvenience of the every-culture structure is the implication that the hero is preordained to undertake and complete the journey of the story. It is inbuilt, like Luke Skywalker, that the protagonist has always had The Force, and needs only the tests of the story in order to be in full possession of that power. Dorothy in *The Wizard of Oz* (script by Noel Langley and Florence Ryerson and Edgar Allan Wolf) always had the ability to go back to Kansas.

> DOROTHY
>
> Oh, will you help me? Can you help me?

> GLINDA
>
> You don't need to be helped any longer. You've always had the power to go back to Kansas.

> DOROTHY
>
> I have?

> SCARECROW
>
> Then why didn't you tell her before?

> GLINDA
>
> Because she wouldn't have believed me. She had to learn it for herself.

TIN MAN
What have you learned, Dorothy?

DOROTHY
Well, I — I think that it — that
it wasn't enough just to want to
see Uncle Henry and Auntie Em —
and it's that — if I ever go
looking for my heart's desire
again, I won't look any further
than my own backyard. Because if
it isn't there, I never really
lost it to begin with! Is that
right?

GLINDA
That's all it is!

SCARECROW
But that's so easy! I should have
thought of it for you.

TIN MAN
I should have felt it in my heart.

GLINDA
No. She had to find it out for
herself. Now, those magic
slippers will take you home in two
seconds.

"**When the legend becomes fact, print the legend.**"

— *The Man Who Shot Liberty Valance*

Long before *The Great Train Robbery* captivated the film audience as the first movie Western in 1903, the making of the American myth was well in progress under the pens of writers like Ned Buntline, Zane Grey, Max Brand, and a select handful of newspapermen who made up the myth and mystique of the American Old West. Ned Buntline himself created the legends of Buffalo Bill Cody, Wild Bill Hickcock, and dozens of other lawmen, gunfighters, gamblers and scoundrels in his popular dime novels of the 19th century. His stories about the cowboy life captivated the imaginations of Eastern city folk, even though the gun-slingin' legends had little to do with the reality of the post–Civil War American West. In truth, the era was populated largely by the dispossessed on the run from the chaos of Reconstruction. There was damned little romance and a lot of sweaty, hard work for the real cowboys who, as often as not, were itinerant southern soldiers, homeless ex-slaves, and the Mexican vaquero descendants of the Conquistadors' cattle herders.

Ned Buntline, a larger-than-life figure himself who'd once been hanged for murder but cut down in time to save his life, was never a storyteller to let facts stand in the way of truth. He recognized that life's daily struggle was no easier for his Eastern readers whose years were mired in swollen tenements and inescapable industrial drudgery. Buntline rewarded his audience with tales of the American West, a wide-open land of renewed national spirit in the aftermath of the bloody Civil War. His cheap paper novels encouraged the vision, despite all first-hand evidence to the contrary, of an independence that was far more evocative than the now rather remote aim of liberation from a tyrannical British government. These sensational adventure books became distinctively American morality plays, where lawmen and gunfighters defined standards of right and wrong, and bull's-eyed the very essence of the American character: that a man of principle, stamina, and strong heart can carve his own way through life, beholden to no one, answerable only to the laws of his God. Eventually, the movies took over where the paperback novels left off, and spread the wonder of the Western myth with shimmering silver clarity.

THE MOMENT OF TRUTH

If there is a single iconographic representation of all that the American Action-Adventure film epitomizes, it is the classic showdown in the dusty street of the Western town. Two men face each other, their hands hovering over their holsters as each scrutinizes his opponent. This moment of truth, of good versus evil, is where the courage of conviction and the power of right is tested. We need only recall Tom Hanks' drawing a bead on the advancing Nazi tank with his sidearm in *Saving Private Ryan* to recognize that the motif is so fraught with significance that it is repeated in one form or another in virtually all Action-Adventure films no matter what content or era is portrayed.

A MAN'S GOTTA DO WHAT A MAN'S GOTTA DO.

Yep. The Western hero is imbued with a commanding sense of honor. Instead of a tradition-bound social code, however, the cowboy's honor arises from the land itself. At times, it even surprises him, seems to rise up from the ground to scratch around inside his skin until he manages to act on the instinctive compulsion to do right by the territory and folks around him.

In *High Noon* (script by Carl Foreman), Will Kane (Gary Cooper) has just turned in his Marshal's badge and married Amy Fowler (Grace Kelly), when he learns that the noon train will bring a gang sworn on personal vengeance. Urged by his friends, Will and Amy head their buckboard toward a new life as far away from killing as they can get. But on the open prairie outside of town, Will grimly reins in the horses.

                    AMY FOWLER KANE
       Why are you stopping?

                    MARSHAL WILL KANE
       It's no good. I've got to
       go back, Amy.

                    AMY FOWLER KANE
       Why?

                    MARSHAL WILL KANE
       This is crazy. I haven't even got
       any guns.

```
              AMY  FOWLER  KANE
Then  let's  go  on.   Hurry.

             MARSHAL  WILL  KANE
No.   That's  what  I've  been
thinking.   They're  making  me  run.
I've  never  run  from  anybody
before.

              AMY  FOWLER  KANE
I  don't  understand  any  of  this.

             MARSHAL  WILL  KANE
Well,  I  haven't  got  time  to  tell
you.

              AMY  FOWLER  KANE
Then  don't  go  back,  Will.

             MARSHAL  WILL  KANE
I've  got  to.   That's  the  whole
thing.
```

THE CLASSIC WESTERN PLOT

For generations, every kid in America has acted out the fundamental Western myth in thousands of suburban backyards, metropolitan playgrounds, inner city alleys, and farmer's fields. In
these make-believe sagas, a hero (sheriff, marshal, or cowboy)

saves the town or the fort or the wagon train from attack by lawless crooks, cattlemen, or Indians in a personal showdown against overwhelming odds to win the thanks of the townsfolk and the love of the beautiful schoolmarm. Acting out the role of the cowboy hero may be a crucial access rite to manhood, branding abstract concepts of the Western myth such as sacrifice, honor, and fair play into the American hide.

A lone stranger who possesses superior skills with a gun, rides into a troubled town, a fragile society of families who are threatened by a group of strong villains who want to destroy their settled, domestic life. The hero is an enigma, for while the society recognizes that he shares the skills of their enemies, he professes the same values as the society itself. The society, therefore, does not trust him enough to welcome him wholeheartedly into their civilized company. He will always stand apart. At the church picnic, he'll be the tall figure with one boot propped against a shade tree, eyes cast down. Sooner or later the schoolmarm will work up enough courage to bring him a plate of food, or the old doc will appoint himself town investigator and sidle up to rummage around in the stranger's background. But even then, though the stranger's smile is warm, his heart isn't that easy to reach. His enigmatic origins finally emerge when the antagonists attempt to force their violent savagery on the tenuous civilization. The taciturn hero proves that he's made of true grit, and single-handedly wallops the bad guys in order to make the land safe for the fragile society that can now take permanent root there.

WHO WAS THAT MASKED MAN?

If this archetypal Western myth seems too simplistic, consider just one theme in this proto-legend that is so noteworthy in the American experience, it appears not only in virtually every Western, but in all their later incarnations as urban Action-Adventure films.

From the very foundation of this country, Americans have shunned effete European or big-city pretense. Our intolerance catalog has long included such refinements as book-learned education, fancy clothes, highbrow music and art, and any form of business that is not look-me-in-the-eye, four-square, on the up-and-up, by-the-handshake, straightforward honest dealing. In the traditional Western the hero may be a stranger to the society, but he shares the values of forthright hard work and an instinctive aversion to affectation and sham. There is nothing more detestable to the hero than a side-windin' snake of a city slicker come out to make fools of honest folks.

The antagonist, therefore, is frequently *not one of us*. He wears inappropriate Eastern suits, speaks a strange-sounding tongue, displays a cultured manner so that you can't read where he's come from, and, above all, has conniving, double-dealing ways. In this one element of the Western myth alone, we are warned to be wary of slick talkers, cautious in our dealings with people who presume to be our betters, and especially to mistrust men who manipulate followers into their bidding through anything less than an honest, democratic free-for-all.

McCabe and Mrs. Miller provides a poignant commentary on this Western distrust of Eastern sharpie greed by turning the conventional Western story on its head. John McCabe, a professional card player, seizes the opportunity to fill a need in a godforsaken mining town by purchasing a couple of prostitutes and setting up a tent canvas brothel-and-bar for the recreation of the miners. Not only do his entrepreneurial efforts pay off, but in short order he also acquires the services of a professional manager in the person of Mrs. Miller who, in turn, attracts more girls and more customers — to the point where John McCabe is a successful businessman beyond anything he'd ever imagined.

But it is exactly his success in the unfamiliar territory of high-profile commerce that is his undoing. The development of a small-time market is one thing, but the making of real money is a province reserved for those who know how to exploit weaknesses. The mining company offers to buy McCabe out, but, puffed up with grandiose dreams of silk-suit success, McCabe not only turns them down, he rubs their face in it with a visit to a local attorney — who promises to fight for his side all the way to the state legislature. Now John McCabe has stepped way out of his boundaries, and there's no time for the niceties of legal channels. Having refused the offer, McCabe's only remaining choice is no longer whether to stay in business, but figuring out how to stay alive. In the end, John McCabe dies alone, unmourned in the drifting snow, a man who ignored the lessons of the myth and tried to transform himself into what we mistrust the most.

The message here is that we are a guileless people, and we must constantly be on our guard against the unprincipled frauds who populate the rest of the world. Our enemies will try to trick us, even in what should be the most straightforward of pursuits, an all-out war. *Battle of the Bulge*, for example, briefly notes the real historical event of a special task force of English-speaking Nazi soldiers assigned to infiltrate the American forces during the Ardennes Offensive.

Whether or not this perception of ourselves as honest, open-hearted palookas is accurate in our current geopolitical circumstances, it was certainly the situation in the hopeful beginnings of our country, when countless predators from both inside and beyond our borders were quite willing to attack by surprise. More important, in the post–Civil War Reconstruction, the expatriate men and women who fled West across the Mississippi, black and white alike, came to reinvent themselves on virgin ground, where they planted a skinned and bleeding foothold of renewed individualism as far away as possible from the deceitfulness of the Yankee carpetbaggers who overran the conquered South. With regard to the *persona* of the Old West, to paraphrase Marshall McLuhan, the migration *is* the myth.

It's your misfortune and none of my own.

Alas, however, in the very act of defeating evil on behalf of the community, the hero cinches his fate in the manifest heartbreak of the American spirit; and it is here that the myth speaks most poignantly of the American dilemma. The clapboard town or besieged wagon train is grateful for the rescue — but the same skills the hero used to secure their salvation are regarded with horror by the citizens as intrinsically hostile talents which threaten the developing embryo of society. The heroic savior is, therefore, rejected by the very same people he saved. The discarded self-sufficient man is condemned to restlessly prowl outside the fringes of the weaker collectives of ordinary human companionship.

Just as the individual experience was expressed in the Western movie, America experienced an analogous predicament as a nation. As American men and women we watched our cultural values portrayed on the screen, and we tried to uphold those same values in the larger sphere of world influence; but we became disillusioned by what seemed to be scant appreciation from the global citizenry.

COWBOY UP — THE MYTH REVISED

To our dismay, by the 1950s, a stalwart hero of principle, stamina, and strong heart was no longer strapping enough to deal with the complexity of post–World War II society. The Western myth itself had to adjust to a more intricate paradigm in order to guide us through our struggles with the confusing morality of the new global pecking order.

Nevertheless, we were certainly not ready to abandon our principles of honor, justice, commitment to a cause, and, above all, loyalty. What failed, we believed, was not our values, but the fact that we squandered those values on the unworthy. We had ignored the lesson of our myth — to stay clear of entanglements with the ineffectual, treacherous, and ungrateful. We sacrificed ourselves in the hopes of being accepted into the cultured community, and found that once we'd done the job for them, the community didn't want us.

For a time, we worked out our disillusionment through revenge. In films like *Winchester 73* and *The Searchers*, the hero abandons the fight on behalf of the weak, ungrateful society, and becomes very much like the men he is chasing, a skilled gunfighter who ignores or breaks the law as one-man judge, jury, and executioner. *The Bravados* with Gregory Peck as Jim Douglass is a case in point, where revenge results in vicious consequences. Douglass returns to his ranch only to discover his house ransacked and his young wife brutally raped and murdered. His neighbor indicates that four men rode through not long before. Without pause, Douglass sets out across the trackless landscape to hunt them down. And hunt them down he does. One by one he stalks and kills his prey, slaughtering each in merciless retribution. But the last man, a young Mexican who's managed to escape across the border to his own wife, takes Douglass by surprise. Rather than outright killing the man who has tormented him for hundreds of miles, the young man is first curious to know why Douglass wants him dead. It is true that he is an unrepentant crook and a thief, and that he even has with him the small bag of gold that was taken from Douglass' house, but he swears he never saw Douglass' wife, much less raped or murdered her. He had taken the bag of gold from the old man on the next ranch over. Suddenly, Douglass is struck by his own hot-headed blunder. It was his very own neighbor, his trusted friend, who stole his money and killed his wife. Of course, the men he has slain may have deserved death for being the outlaws they were, but not for committing the acts for which they had been wrongly accused. The betrayal was not theirs, but his — for not remaining true to the heart of justice.

Just as the hero in these Western stories learns that revenge is hollow, so, too, was the myth redrawn in the post–World War II era. We turned from focusing on self-righteous anger to a renewal of our founding principles. We regrouped back behind our secure, reinforced value of self-reliance, trusting only those who had absolutely proven to be, like us, willing to sacrifice their lives for a goal.

"WE NEVER SLEEP."

— MOTTO OF THE PINKERTON DETECTIVE AGENCY

After World War II, our heroes were far more guarded, their senses honed to a vigilant edge and ready for the slightest sign of weakness or deceit. No more did we see the big-hearted, youthful cowboy with the fast guns. Our heroes were straight-razor stropped, venom-spitting professionals. By the mid-1950s, the Western became the story of hard-bitten *professional* gun-slingers. On television, programs like *Gunsmoke* and *Have Gun Will Travel* took on the badge of Adult Westerns, where a mortal and decidedly cynical hero was the defender of law and order.

In movies, the professional's cynicism makes him, as often as not, a reluctant hero. John Wayne's Rooster Cogburn in *True Grit* (script by Marguerite Roberts) has no intention at all of helping a brash young woman, Mattie Ross (Kim Darby) track down her father's murderer. The promise of money appears to rouse him from his inertia, though, even if the cantankerous old lawman is harnessed on one side with the exasperating girl (a harbinger of the upheaval to come) and on the other with a fresh-faced, wholesome Texas Ranger (Glen Campbell), who's a genuine throwback to the white-hat cowboys of the classic Western myth. Remarkably, these three unlikely saddle pals manage to track down the bad guys and exact justice *without* vengeance.

```
              ROOSTER COGBURN
        I mean to kill you in one minute,
        Ned, or see you hanged in Ft.
        Smith at Judge Parker's
        convenience.  Which'll it be?


              "LUCKY" NED PEPPER
        I call that bold talk for a
        one-eyed fat man.


              ROOSTER COGBURN
        Fill your hand, you
        son-of-a-bitch.
```

Ned Pepper (Robert Duvall) has crossed the line. Not only has he defied Cogburn's authority by flouting the law, but now he's insulted the authentic embodiment of that law. *Individual worth* has secured a place in the myth. Rooster takes on the Pepper gang all by himself in one of the most majestic gunfights ever filmed.

No Fear — The Professional Hero

No longer the guileless adolescent, the American cowboy has been bucked off once too often. No more unselfish giving. In films like *The Magnificent Seven*, *The Great Northfield Minnesota Raid*, *The Wild Bunch*, and *Butch Cassidy and the Sundance Kid*, the heroes have been discarded by a contemporary Western society that has succumbed to the stingy, conniving commercialism of the East.

The heroes, therefore, reject the hypocritical, carnival huckster mentality, and find mutual respect, honor, and trust within their own elite group of peers with unique skills, as does a group of outcasts in *The Professionals* (script by Richard Brooks).

```
               RICO FARDAN
          We promised Mr. Grant that we
          would do the job.


               BILL DOLWORTH
          My word ain't worth a plug nickel
          to men like Grant.


               RICO FARDAN
          You gave your word to me.
```

These heroes derive their values from their fundamental *sense of right* as expressed in their associations with each other. They are motivated by professional loyalty, and although they may inevitably act to defend a principle shared by the ideal society, it is done in defense of their professional colleagues, even at the loss of their own lives.

In *The Professionals*, Lee Marvin is Henry "Rico" Fardan, an ex-Army officer now cheapened to the shameful job of a drummer for automatic weapons. But Marvin receives a summons from a wealthy rancher, Mr. J. W. Grant (Ralph Bellamy), who engages Rico to rescue his young wife Maria (Claudia Cardinale) from her kidnapper, the bandit Jesus Raza (Jack Palance).

```
                    GRANT
          Jesus.   What  a  name  for  the
          bloodiest  cutthroat  in  Mexico.
```

Rico agrees to accept the job, but only if he can hand-pick his team of professional colleagues. Grant gives Rico his enthusiastic blessing, as well as the services of his private railroad car, and a promise of $10,000 per man when his wife is returned. Rico calls together the professionals, an assortment of society's rejects who are not past their prime, but past their time. They eke out life on the disillusioned fringes, plying skills uncalled for in a civilized world. The bounty hunter Jake Sharp (Woody Strode), the wrangler Hans Ehrengard (Robert Ryan), and the dynamite specialist Bill Dolworth (Burt Lancaster), are men united by their respect for each other's skills, bonded to one another outside a society that no longer needs or accepts them. And Rico's professionals fulfill their assigned task, riding deep into the Mexican desert to rescue Mr. Grant's prize. However, along the way, we learn that their bond of loyalty once extended to the bandito, Jesus, Raza himself. In fact, Rico and Bill Dolworth fought side-by-side with Raza during the Mexican revolution.

They also discover that Mrs. Grant was not kidnapped at all, but willingly ran away from her forced marriage to be with her life-long lover Jesus Raza. Nevertheless, the professionals have a contract with Grant and intend to carry out their half of the bargain. On the headlong return across the border, however, Burt Lancaster holds back in a narrow pass in order to slow Raza's pursuit while his colleagues escape. During the standoff with Raza, the two former allies recall a time when their skills had meaning, when they acted for *ideals* rather than money.

```
                    JESUS RAZA
          To die for money is foolish.


                   BILL DOLWORTH
          To die for a woman is more
          foolish.  Any woman.


                    JESUS RAZA
          But she is my woman.  Now and for
          always.
```

                    BILL DOLWORTH
Nothing is for always. Ask Fiero.
Ask Francisco. Ask those in the
Cemetery of Nameless Men.

                    JESUS RAZA
They died for what they believed.

                    BILL DOLWORTH
The Revolution? When the shooting
stops and the dead are buried, and
the politicians take over, it all
adds up to one thing. A lost
cause.

                    JESUS RAZA
You want perfection or nothing.
You are too romantic, compadre.
La Revolucion is like a great love
affair. In the beginning, she is
a goddess. A holy cause. But
every love affair has a terrible
enemy.

                    BILL DOLWORTH
Time.

                    JESUS RAZA
We see her as she is. La
Revolucion is not a goddess, but a
whore. Never saintly. Never

```
perfect.  So we run away.  Find
another lover.  Quick, sordid
affairs.  Lust without love.
Passion, but no compassion.
Without love, without a cause, we
are nothing.  We stay because we
believe.  We leave because we are
disillusioned.  We come back
because we are lost.  We die
because we are committed.
```

Even as the two adversaries take aim at one another, their hearts remember a time when a man fought for moral dignity. It is this kind of struggle for integrity, absent from the earlier Westerns where characters were merely good or bad, that provides the keystone for all later Action-Adventure films, and distinguishes the *best* of the genre from the thoughtless spectacles of brutality that are dumped into today's syndication theaters.

In the end, Dolworth's conversation with Raza is the key that leads each member of Rico's band of professionals to recover his own self-worth, even at the sacrifice of the $10,000 apiece reward money. In the face of the guns wielded by J. W. Grant's syco-phants, the professionals return Maria to Raza and his trackless desert. Tomorrow, or the next day, or the next, each man may revert to the life of a social outcast; but in this moment, they have justly fought for possession of their own true souls.

IS THIS THE END OF RICO?

— *THE PUBLIC ENEMY*

As the urbanization of America increased, so did the aspiration for metropolitan heroes, especially among our nation's immigrants. They experienced the same daily struggle for personal integrity, and felt the same scorn from a thankless society that motivated the Western professional heroes. So just as the Civil War spawned the outcasts who would become the stewards of Old West values, Prohibition generated the champions of the inner city — the Tommy-gun gangsters.

In *The Public Enemy*, *Scarface*, *Little Caesar*, and the like, James Cagney, Edward G. Robinson, and Paul Muni portrayed the stand-up tough-guys who took it on the chin to resist the overwhelming forces of corrupt city cops and ambitious politicos. They were the little man's heroes, and they exhibited much the same spirit of individual achievement as did the Old West cowboy: the ability to get up and do what had to be done without ever knuckling under. They may have been crooks, but they were *our* crooks doing battle against the tub-thumping moralists, bamboozling bankers, and double-dealing politicians who tried to tell *us* how to live our lives.

The pinnacle of the gangster movie, and the most sophisticated expression of the gangster as hero for the common man, was actually achieved long after the demise of the genre itself. The superb, watershed film *Bonnie and Clyde* (script by Robert Benton & David Newman) combined all the elements of the Depression-era stories into a lyrical vision of romantic scope that elevated a couple of dust bowl stick-up artists into modern cinema idols. In one poignant scene, Bonnie and Clyde practice shooting at bottles propped on the fence of an abandoned farm house. Nailed to the door is the sign, "Property of Midlothian Citizens Bank — Trespassers will be prosecuted." As Bonnie fires, a farmer scuffles up from the front of the house where an old Negro man waits beside an Oakie car packed with belongings, a woman with a baby in her arms, and a small boy.

                    FARMER
          Hi do.

Clyde whirls around, aims at the farmer.

                    FARMER
          No sir... no sir. You all go
          right ahead. Used to be my place.
          Not anymore. Bank took it.

                    BONNIE
          Well, that's a pitiful shame.

                    FARMER
          Me and him put in the years here.
          Yessir. So you all go right
          ahead. We just come by for a last
          look.

He turns away toward the car as Clyde spins and fires three fast shots into the foreclosure sign, then offers the gun to the farmer. He takes aim at the sign and fires, then breaks into a huge grin.

> FARMER
> Hey, Davis! Come on over here.

Bonnie hands her gun to the old Negro, who slowly raises it to fire at a window. The farmer fires again, shattering a second window. He nods, and Davis fires again. None of them can keep from laughing as the farmer returns the guns to Clyde.

> FARMER
> Much obliged. I'm Otis Harrison.
> And this here's Davis. We worked
> this place.

> CLYDE
> This's Miss Bonnie Parker. And
> I'm Clyde Barrow. We rob banks.

For a while, the gangster overtook the cowboy as the folk hero who defended the rights of the little guy against the avarice of City Hall and Wall Street. These societal loose cannons were, as often as not, immigrants, or the sons of immigrants, who wasted no time in grasping the truly important urban value of money.

Money, we understood, provided power, and lack of power was the one thing that the tenement residents and rural sharecroppers had in common. Nor was this the first set of gangsters to capture the public imagination. In an earlier economic depression, the brothers James, Younger, and Dalton became legendary figures, mobsters of the plains who defied Wells Fargo and the Pinkertons with the same flamboyance imparted to the movie versions of Al Capone, Pretty Boy Floyd and John Dillinger. Metropolis and farmland alike developed their own models of the gangster hero, and swapped the cowboy's good-natured grin for a defiant smirk.

Rats, Gats, and Roscoes

The gangster films also set the fashion for a new component of the Action-Adventure film. In the Westerns, the robbers always rushed out of the bank firing their guns in the air until the terrified townsfolk dived out of sight long enough for the bad guys to jump on their horses for the getaway. Naturally, the cowboy hero rounded up the posse for a galloping pursuit, riding hell-for-leather, six-guns blazing, in a chase across the prairie. For the most part, the action remained a contest between the defenders and the invaders of society in which the local residents were rarely in direct danger. In fact, in the earliest Westerns, an understood code among the crooks kept the killing limited to those who would stand in their way, and a possible female hostage now and then. But refinements in the technology of indiscriminate death fostered by World War I cultivated an equal lack of restraint on the civilian streets. By the 1920s, the

Thompson submachine gun found its way into the hands of hoodlums and law enforcement officers alike. The tommy gun became such a fixture in movies that it's hard to imagine a gangster picture without the familiar drum of a chattering .45 automatic poked out the back door of a black sedan as it roars around the corner. The wholesale broadcast of hot lead at cops and innocent bystanders alike that began with the Prohibition rumrunners has escalated steadily ever since into an ongoing hardware war of Action-Adventure firepower.

With the attack on Pearl Harbor, the public rallied around a revived patriotism. America refocused its industrial, economic, and moral energies, and the gangster film quickly faded away. Elements of the genre soon emigrated through the stylistic *film noir* to take up residence in the Detective and Thriller film genres. In short order, the gangster's stick-the-finger-to-authority defiance resonated with the can-do insolence of returning G.I.s to spawn a new Action-Adventure hero who could whip the world.

THEM'S FIGHTIN' WORDS

So the American myth comes almost full circle, from a legendary hero endowed with strength, innate goodness, and *aw shucks ma'am* purity, through a cynical destructive force not yet willing to give up his belief in the fundamental principle of what's *right*, to the self-confident, home-grown champion who'll make up his own rules, and gladly blast hell, high water, and tin-horn officials right out of his way to put his own life on the line if he's decided in his heart that the cause is just. Evil may have cunning intellect, money, powerful resources, and fancy speech, but on our side we've got American kick-ass impertinence, and no-fear swagger. Evil doesn't stand a chance.

THE BIRTHRIGHT OF ACTION-ADVENTURE

THE WESTERN PARADIGM — The outcast drifter uses his martial skills to save a fragile society by upholding law and order, thereby winning the gratitude of the townsfolk, and the love of the schoolmarm.

ALLIED TO:

THE GANGSTER PARADIGM — The inner-city refugee scorns the repressive morality of traditional society in favor of the raw, personal clout of guns and wealth, thereby winning the admiration of the common man and the love of the girl who's too good for him.

BECOMES:

THE URBAN ACTION-ADVENTURE PARADIGM — The insolent rouge cop fights outside the edge of the law to uphold the values of justice on behalf of a vulnerable society, thereby winning civic respect and the love of the upwardly mobile female executive.

Scribble Exercise:

❏ **Who was your favorite Action-Adventure movie hero before you were twelve years old? What qualities did that hero embody?**

- Physical strength?

- Courage?

- Independence?

- Contempt for wrongdoing?

- Absolute honesty?

- Emotional detachment?

❏ **What Action-Adventure movie hero has made the greatest impression on you as an adult? Does your adult hero demonstrate any of the qualities of:**

- Compassion for the weak?

- A sense of community?

- Vulnerability to emotion?

- Willingness to compromise?

❏ **In what everyday circumstances do you try to behave like your Action-Adventure hero?**

CHAPTER 5

ACTION-ADVENTURE STRUCTURE

AND, SO, THEN...

When you experience a sudden, extraordinary but unanticipated event such as an automobile accident, a burglary to your home, or a natural disaster like an earthquake or tornado, you undoubtedly find yourself talking about the incident for days, weeks or even months afterward. After a while, you become fed up with listening to yourself, but you feel compelled to button-hole passersby like the Ancient Mariner [3] to repeat your tale over and over again. Yet, with each telling, the story takes on a faintly altered shape, the thousands of details from yesterday's recall become mere nuances in today's performance, and now and then a glimmer of insight flashes in a blink, before the words escape your mouth.

You are *narrating* your life, making sense out of the haphazard by arranging the indiscriminate events into a *story*. Furthermore, you *must* do it. As a species, humans are obligated to find meaning in the tangle of stimuli that we interpret as reality. The human perceptual system is bombarded as the countless minutiae of an event compete for our awareness. All

---

[3] "The Rime of the Ancient Mariner" by Samuel Taylor Coleridge.

of them push, shove, and elbow to the front of the line in "Me first!" pandemonium. After a while, though, not unlike the doorman at a trendy nightclub, we begin to reject some of the applicants for our attention, and cut the line down to only those hopefuls who seem to be the most influential. Pretty soon, the sheer numbers have been cut back until there are fewer details competing for our attention. Now we can make some real choices. Based on what we believe to be similarities in shape, size, color, or even time, we start structuring the remaining stimuli into patterns — big, small, fast, slow, up, down, etc. Sure enough, some of those patterns appear to be larger or more important, so they come to the front of our conscious narration while other groupings of apparently less substance recede into the background. At this level, we take on the most human function of the perceptual process — we assign *meaning* to the limited features that remain. Based on our own experiences, behavior, and attitudes we give the event a significance that fits within our value system.

"PREDICTION IS VERY DIFFICULT. ESPECIALLY WHEN IT CONCERNS THE FUTURE."

— NIELS BOHR

Like life, the cinematic experience also floods our senses, but the distinctive difference is that film overwhelms us with super-stimuli, saturated color, and digital sound — a sixty-foot-tall *hyper-reality* — so that the darkened movie theater provides an infinite gateway into a world that is not at all like the streets we left outside. This altered world engulfs us with intense emotional, intellectual, and even physical signals that can produce not only emotional and psychological responses, but physiological effects such as increased heart rate, dizziness, and even nausea.

Of course, like the stimuli of "real" life, it is quite possible to throw images and sounds at the audience more or less at random. Because we are human beings, we are bound to make some kind of sense out of the jumble. There is a film editing phenomenon called the *Kuleshov Effect*, named for the pioneer Russian film-maker Lev Kuleshov, that demonstrates how powerful this human need to make sense out of the random is. Kuleshov intercut three copies of exactly the same shot of an actor's face with three separate images: a bowl of hot soup; a dead woman lying in a coffin; and a little girl playing with a teddy bear. When the three clips were shown to three different audiences, the viewers praised the actor's portrayal of a hungry man dreaming of food, his deep sorrow over the death of his mother, and his delight at watching his daughter play.

Screenplays, then, need to be a highly structured narrative form in order to make certain that every second of screen time counts in the telling of a story. The screenwriter must very skillfully choose, from all the possible actions that might occur, only those events that have a direct impact on the cause-and-effect story of the crucial decision that the main character makes, and the resulting action that launches that character's world on a new course. Careful structure produces a forceful screenplay plot that is not real life, but freeze-dried life — not reality, but reality made more potent and dramatic, because all the irrelevant gaps have been removed.

More than any other genre the Action-Adventure hurtles us into this hyper-reality because it is filled with actions by remarkable characters in extraordinary events that have astonishing consequences. The physical surroundings might be recognizable as familiar terra firma, but the ordeals encountered — war, catastrophe, social upheaval, deadly force — transform those surroundings from the stuff of our personal everyday existence. The screenwriter's exacting selection of events and artful compression of time, then, is especially demanding if the script is going to sustain the audience's belief in that exaggerated world.

Nonetheless, although rigorous structure is surely the most crucial element of a screenplay, even the most well thought-out choices of significant events will not, by themselves, make a convincing story. We can give an account of the proceedings of the D-Day invasion of Normandy: catalog the numbers of ships, men, and materiel; count the dead; and map the ground gained. All of these facts are noteworthy, and taken as a whole, the mere recitation of the data is capable of bringing tears to the eyes of

anyone who witnessed such heroic carnage. But the facts themselves are devoid of emotion, and the assembled quantities do not
even come close to giving us the narrative experience that a good
storyteller can produce. No amount of tears shed in remem-
brance can approach the magnitude of emotion wrung from the
hearts of an audience sharing the concentrated experience of that
event, even a re-created experience. Are these *real* events? Of
course not. No one in the audience is going to die. No one is
going to be disemboweled or blinded or maimed. No one is going
to feel lungs burst for air or legs turn to jelly with fear. Stories
are not actuality; they are a simulacrum, an interpretation of the
stimuli we experience as reality.

Of course, there are stylistic ways to rearrange the beginning,
middle, and end to achieve an effect in the telling of a story.
Particularly in a detective genre story such as *The Usual Suspects*,
it may even help to engage the audience by confusing the relationship between the beginning, middle and end. No matter
how the writer ultimately arranges time and events to have a
particular influence, however, the actual actions of the story
must happen on an observable, chronological scale that can be
reconstructed in a coherent cause-and-effect sequence. If the
events cannot be arranged in such a rational order, then there are
serious gaps in the story logic that will ultimately be unsettling to
an audience.

Obviously, skillful writers always use a certain amount of sleight
of hand when arranging narrative events. The logic of a story is
never so absolutely foolproof that it would withstand the tests of
evidence. Nevertheless, the reasonable structure of the story

must always appear to be flawless to the audience, even if they are later struck by what Alfred Hitchcock called "refrigerator logic," that sudden realization while pouring a glass of milk before bed that the protagonist *couldn't* have known about the gun because...

"WRITING IS EASY. ALL YOU DO IS STARE AT A BLANK SHEET OF PAPER UNTIL DROPS OF BLOOD FORM ON YOUR FOREHEAD."

— GENE FOWLER, U.S. JOURNALIST AND AUTHOR

The logic of good story structure, then, is more than meticulously planned events. It is the underlying support of <u>authenticity</u> that makes those events the bearers of truth. What distinguishes a compelling Action-Adventure feature film from a dime-a-dozen shoot-'em-up is the care and skill the screenwriter takes to bring the audience along with the essential motivations of the story. It is all too easy for writers to become enamored of exotic locations, or filigrees of character (such as eye patches, foreign dialects, and odd quirks of behavior), or convoluted Rube Goldberg action sequences requiring feats of logistics that would stagger NASA. But as attractive as these gimmicks may seem, every glittery overindulgence comes at the high cost of reassuring the audience's trust in the *truth of the story* on the screen. Audience members can only allow themselves to be frightened, exhilarated, distraught, and courageous because they trust that the writer knows exactly where the story is going, even if they don't. In return, the writer must make certain that the audience is always located in the story, not only in time and space, but in the significance of the underlying meaning.

In the care of a master screenwriter, the reader has confidence in the storyteller precisely because of the tiny brush strokes of authenticity. There is an ambience in Robert Towne's script for *Chinatown* that is elegantly transposed to the screen. The landscape is parched, with bleached white buildings that dominate the city and, more and more, bear down on Jake Gittes, the nosy private eye who almost loses his nose. A good screenwriter uses the cunning inventions of language on the page to create the grace notes of a thematic concert.

BEGINNING   ⇨   MIDDLE   ⇨   END

The Action-Adventure genre is itself the most honest of film forms, inasmuch as it is the American morality play about the triumph of good over evil. Consequently, the more this uncomplicated thesis is obscured with stylistic embellishment, the more it weakens both the moral and emotional impact of an Action-Adventure drama. The storytelling of Action-Adventure is, therefore, straightforward, four-square, up-and-up like its parent myth, and relatively undemanding of anything more than the audience's unconditional devotion.

Unconditional devotion? Not an easy goal by any means. This simple requirement is what *Screenwriting 101* discusses as an *Audience-Focused Sequence*, an interpretation of the three-act, beginning, middle, and end structure as a way of crafting emotional responses from the audience.

> **AUDIENCE-FOCUSED SEQUENCE**
>
> | Beginning | Middle | End |
> |---|---|---|
> | **ATTRACTION** | **ANTICIPATION** | **SATISFACTION** |
> | Act I | Act II | Act III |

1. **ATTRACTION** — As much as we might like to think our fascinating characters are as intriguing to the audience as they are to us as writers, the fact is that the audience is not so much interested in the character as in the predicament the character is facing. Of course, it is necessary to have a main character that the audience responds to, but there will be time enough as the drama progresses to explore the conflict between that character's self-concept and inner need. In the beginning, what the audience really wants to know is — What is this story *about*, and how the hell is the main character going to get out of this mess? *The Guns of Navarone* (script by Carl Foreman) is set up with a statement of the *impossible mission* that must be accomplished. A brace of gigantic naval guns entrenched on a Greek island must be destroyed if the lives of thousands of British landing troops are going to be saved.

> SQUADRON LEADER HOWARD BARNSBY
> It can't be done. Not from the
> air, anyway.

> COMMODORE JAMES JENSEN
> You're quite sure about that,
> Squadron Leader? This is
> important.

> SQUADRON LEADER HOWARD BARNSBY
> So's my life. To me anyway. And
> the lives of these jokers here.
> And the eighteen men we lost
> tonight. Look, Sir, first you've
> got that bloody old fortress on
> top of that bloody cliff. Then
> you've got the bloody cliff
> overhang. Can't even see the
> bloody cave, let alone the bloody
> guns. At any rate, we haven't got
> a bloody bomb big enough to smash
> that bloody rock. And that's the
> bloody truth, Sir.

2. **ANTICIPATION** — The screenwriter cranks up the tension of the story by escalating the conflict between the main character and the antagonist, increasing the audience's expectations that more and more interesting things will happen. However, these interesting things aren't merely disjointed bits of physical

action. No tension is created by action alone. No matter how frenetic they may be, action sequences such as car crashes, gunfights, etc. are dramatically inert. Nothing happens until the action produces a result. Tension builds because the action *did not* produce the result that the characters, and the audience, *expected* to happen. Therefore the characters must make new decisions to predict unknown results. It is the anxiety of the unknown that creates excitement for the audience.

In *The Professionals*, Rico and his hand-picked team manage to set up diversions around Jesus Raza's stronghold so that the bandits believe they are being attacked by *Federales*. In the midst of the confusion, Rico and Dolworth will slip into Maria Grant's quarters to kidnap her and return her to their employer. But while they wait for exactly the right moment, Rico and Dolworth are stunned to see Raza enter Maria's bedroom, where it is clear that the captor and his hostage are anything but antagonistic to each other.

<pre>
                    DOLWORTH
          Amigo, we've been had.
</pre>

At this point, everything the main characters have believed, and everything the audience has understood about the story changes radically. Rico's professionals could simply call off the mission and return across the border — but that would be an action in direct contradiction to the nature of the characters. Instead, they elect to fulfill their contract anyway. It is the sense of duty to perform the job *professionally* that sets up the subsequent action of the story, as well as the satisfaction of a worthy resolution to the conflict.

3. **Satisfaction** — Because of the failure of the action to produce the expected results, and because the antagonist is, by nature, stronger than the main character, the hero must overcome internal obstacles such as his own fears in order to resolve the external dilemma that attracted the audience in Act I. Only in this way can the audience anticipation built up in Act II be satisfied. Viewers have now experienced a complete story that, unlike the humdrum chaos of life, has a clear beginning, middle, and end, and makes sense out of capricious reality.

The ironic final scene of *Full Metal Jacket* (script by Michael Herr & Stanley Kubrick) silhouettes the Marine platoon against the raging fires of a burnt-out city at night, their voices raised in mocking commentary on the living hell that surrounds them.

```
          MARINE PLATOON (V.O.)
     Who's the leader of the club
     that's made for you and me?
     M-I-C-K-E-Y M-O-U-S-E.
     Hey there. Hi there. Ho there.
     You're as welcome as can be.
     M-I-C-K-E-Y M-O-U-S-E.
     Mickey Mouse. Mickey Mouse.
     Forever let us hold our banner
     high. High. High. High.  Come
     along and sing a song and
     join the jamboree. M-I-C-K-E-Y
     M-O-U-S-E.
```

77

"ALL MY LIFE I'VE LOOKED AT WORDS AS THOUGH I WERE SEEING THEM FOR THE FIRST TIME."

— ERNEST HEMINGWAY

Often carelessly maligned as a prescriptive blueprint, essential screenplay structure is, in fact, no tedious, unvarying march, but a gavotte of rhythms tapped, tangoed, boogie-woogied and stomped onto the soul of every audience member. Focusing on *attraction*, *anticipation*, and *satisfaction*, the screenwriter can now transform these broad divisions of Act I Act II, and Act III into smaller units that will establish a story progression for the audience. In the same sense that a trial attorney requires evidence to prove an argument, or a scientist must have research data to back up a hypothesis, the screenwriter must bring the audience along in legs of the journey through the plot from beginning to end in order to impart to them the overall *encounter* with the drama.

THE ORDER OF BATTLE

The structural units that make up the three acts of drama are contained in *all* genres. Some stories put more weight on one or another of the components, and the precise sequential order is of less concern than the totality of their effect, but these elements make up the irreducible armature on which all good stories are sculpted. Nevertheless, textbook structure alone will not produce a great screenplay. Just as a mason can use identical construction techniques but employ wholly different materials to achieve different effects with brick, marble, sandstone or river rock, so, too, the characteristics that underlie story structure generate very different *spaces* for narratives to inhabit. For this reason, the following elements bear different names from their counterparts in *Screenwriting 101: The Essential Craft Of Feature Film Writing*. Both lists identify exactly the same structural functions, but the *qualities* of the events outlined below are unique to the Action-Adventure genre.

❏ **BRIEFING** Certain events occurred in the past that established the conditions of the current story. Because the plots of Action-Adventure stories are ordinarily not very complicated, there is generally very little Briefing required to get started. Often, only a line or two of dialogue is enough to establish the essential problem and the necessity for doing something about it. In the beginning, the audience needs to know why things are about to happen in order for the story to begin. There will be time enough later in the story to add more background if necessary. In *The Towering Inferno*, Fire Chief Michael O'Hallorhan (Steve McQueen) proclaims, "There's a fire up there! We gotta get those people down!" That is all the audience needs to know to get the story rolling. The information that the fire in the high-rise is the result of cutting corners on building codes does not appear until much later in the film.

James Cameron uses the simplest possible Briefing technique in *Terminator 2: Judgment Day*. The opening voiceover narration flatly states that there's a bad terminator coming to kill John Conner and a good terminator coming to rescue him. According to John's mother Sarah, "It was only a question of which one got to him first."

The most awkward way to brief the audience is with a flash-back narrative. Although flashbacks can be used to good effect, most often beginning screenwriters seem to need to stop the story that the audience is watching in order to go back in time for a lengthy exposition on the details of prior circumstances. Of course, by the time this interruption is finished, the audience no longer remembers the story they are supposed to be watching. A skillful screenwriter keeps the Briefing on a strictly need-to-know basis:

• Does the plot unconditionally require that the audience have this data in order for the action of the story to begin?

• If the data is required, what is the easiest access to the material? Can the brief be piggybacked onto story action?

❑ **SKELETON PACK** No matter how courageous, the protagonist always carries a skeleton backpack into combat. There is some incomplete quality that is going to be tested by the action of the drama. It is a unique quality of movies that they cast us into the reality of the picture in such a way that we feel the tribulations of the main character. The skeleton we sense may be a missing personal quality such as physical courage, but, more likely, the skeleton is just that: a framework without substance, values that have never been tested under fire. It is only now, through conflict with the external antagonist, that these values will be called into question. One appeal of the Action-Adventure as a morality play, is that it not only clearly states the test of good vs. evil, but because of our attachment to the protagonist, we must also take stock of our own values.

In *Zulu* (script by John Prebble and Cy Endfield), for instance, Michael Caine's Lt. Gonville Bromhead is an effete gentleman officer, a product of his upper-class upbringing, who is unpredictably confronted with having to live up to the expressed stiff-upper-lip ideals of his social caste against an onslaught from thousands of disciplined Zulu warriors. It is something of a revelation that the inexperienced lieutenant not only carries out his duty, but he does so with admirable leadership and outstanding valor. Yet, it is not until the aftermath of victory, as Bromhead and his co-commander Lt. John Chard (Stanley Baker) survey a rampart of bodies, that Bromhead's resolute upper-class code is tested by waist-deep, disembowled carnage, and he reveals the feelings behind his intrepid courage.

                    LT. JOHN CHARD
          Well, you've fought your first
          action.

                    LT. GONVILLE BROMHEAD
          Does everyone feel like this
          afterwards?

                    LT. JOHN CHARD
          How do you feel?

81

                    LT. GONVILLE BROMHEAD
          Sick.

                    LT. JOHN CHARD
          You have to be alive to feel sick.

                    LT. GONVILLE BROMHEAD
          You asked me, I told you. There's
          something else. I feel ashamed.
          Was that how it was for you? The
          first time?

                    LT. JOHN CHARD
          The first time? You think I could
          stand this butcher's yard more
          than once?

The Guns of Navarone uses a different device to portray the moral battle that rages inside Gregory Peck's Capt. Keith Mallory. As a skilled mountain climber, Mallory is recruited into an elite commando group that will assault the impregnable Nazi gun emplacement on an occupied Greek island. Mallory's sole job is to lead the group up the sheer cliff so that they can surreptitiously enter the town. However, the commando leader Maj. Roy Franklin (Anthony Quayle) breaks his leg on the ascent. Mallory must now take over leadership and, what's more, decide what to do with his seriously injured friend Franklin. Alistair MacLean, who wrote the novel, and screenwriter Carl Foreman use two opposing characters to portray the skeleton that Mallory bears — does war permit men of good intent to forego the ordinary restraints of morality in order to defeat an immoral enemy? On one side there is the pragmatic Greek Col. Andrea Stavros (Anthony Quinn) who accepts death as a straightforward consequence of the fight for a cause. On the other is Corporal Miller (David Niven), a self-professed non-participant with a commitment only to a person rather than a principle.

```
          CPL. MILLER
For all we know he's hurt inside,
too.  He needs proper medical
attention.

          CAPT. KEITH MALLORY
What do you suggest?

          CPL. MILLER
If we leave him here, the Germans
will take care of him.  They have
to.

          PRIVATE "BUTCHER" BROWN
They'll get him to a hospital,
sir.  If he doesn't get
sulfanilamide for this leg of his,
he doesn't stand a chance.

          CAPT. KEITH MALLORY
Naturally, you all think a great
deal of Major Franklin.  So do I.
```

We have two choices. We can take
him with us, and if he doesn't get
help soon, he'll die. Or, we can
leave him here, in which case
he'll tell the Germans everything
they want to know.

                CPL. MILLER
Roy! Never.

              CAPT. KEITH MALLORY
He might not be able to help
himself. They have other drugs
besides sulfa. All they have to
do is shoot him full of
scopolamine, and he'll tell them
our whole plan. In detail.

              COL. ANDREA STAVROS
There is, of course, a third
choice. One bullet now. Better
for him. Better for us. You take
that man along, you endanger us
all.

❏ **INITIAL CONTACT** The Action-Adventure begins on a day when
a threat directly challenges the society to which the main character
belongs. Moreover, the protagonist must inescapably and
personally take immediate, decisive action against the menace,
or society will suffer grave consequences. In the original *Die*

Hard, Det. John McClane (Bruce Willis) is the only character in the Nakatomi building who is not immediately under
the control of Hans Gruber (Alan Rickman) and his gang. Now,
if John were an ordinary man, he would probably do what all
of us with any sense would do — hide and wait out the crisis.
However, McClane is no ordinary man. In the first place,
John McClane is a cop. By training, by sense of duty, and by
the personality that made him choose to be a police officer,
McClane cannot do *nothing*. He must respond to the threat.
In the second place, McClane is also the estranged husband
of a woman who, along with her colleagues, is threatened by
cold-blooded killers. McClane has no choice — he must
take on the duty of carrying the fight to the enemy.

❏ **IMPOSSIBLE MISSION** The urgency of the Initial Contact
focuses the main character on a specific target, an Impossible
Mission to destroy a heavily fortified enemy outpost, defend a
position against the onslaught of superior numbers, or possibly
to capture an object or territory. The precise target may or
may not seem to be important initially, but it is a crucial link
in the security of the threatened society. Indiana Jones is sent
in search of the fabled Ark of the Covenant. However, the
relic itself, in spite of its mighty power, is not the worthy goal.
Detached from the context of World War II and the Nazi
obsession to acquire the artifact for their own evil purposes,
Indiana's quest would be nothing more than a mercenary lust
for personal glory. It is the race to keep the mystical power
out of the wrong hands that makes the goal worthwhile.

In fact, the protagonist's target may even change over the course of the drama. The original goal may be false, even selfish, but the morality of Action-Adventure demands that at the end of the day, the main character achieve a *worthy* goal. Michael Douglas' Jack Colton in *Romancing the Stone* is a roguish loner who couldn't care less about Joan Wilder's (Kathleen Turner) predicament except as a means to get his mitts on the treasure of the *el corazón* emerald. In the course of the drama, however, Jack's goal shifts from selfish avarice to worthy concern for the safety of Joan and her sister because he has fallen in love with Joan. Of course, in the spirit of comic Action-Adventure, he actually manages to get both the money and the girl, but there's no pretense that *Romancing the Stone* is real life.

❏ **RECONNOITER** If acquiring the target goal were easy, there would be no story. In Action-Adventure, even though more or less immediate action is called for, the first thing the main character must do is devise a strategy for achieving the goal. Resources, equipment, and possibly professional team members have to be assembled. In fact, for many Action-Adventure films, this period of preparation is not only vital, but occupies an amount of time that would be unbalanced in other forms of drama.

In *The Dirty Dozen*, for instance, the bulk of the film is about preparing a bunch of criminal misfits to act together as a military unit in order to achieve the goal of blowing away as many of the Nazi brass as possible. This period of preparation builds tension during the state of siege, the Narrative Trajectory that is the overarching framework of Action-Adventure.

❏ **TARGET ACQUISITION** Drama is conflict. Without someone acting against the main character, there is no *anticipation* build-up for the audience. There must be an outside force, an antagonist who is meaner, more powerful, and has more resources than the main character. It is the antagonist's job to prevent the main character from reaching the goal, because the antagonist wants either the same goal or a mutually exclusive goal. Even though Action-Adventure characters are relatively straightforward compared to, for instance, more multifaceted characters in dramas dealing with the search for personal integrity, they should not be one-dimensional cardboard figures. This is especially true of Action-Adventure antagonists. Too often screenwriters make the mistake of painting broad, rather silly antagonists who are nothing more than slavering psychopaths with nothing else to motivate them than amorphous evil. Consider that for the protagonist to take steps to achieve a worthy goal, he must encounter an opponent who is worth not only his supreme efforts but, more important, will force the main character to come to grips with a crucial personal issue. In *Die Hard: With a Vengeance* (script by Jonathan Hensleigh), Simon Peter Gruber and his band of former East German Stasi agents have a very real, almost sympathetic goal.

> SIMON PETER GRUBER
> Yesterday, we were an army with no country. Tomorrow, we have to decide which country we want to buy.

❑ **DEBRIEFING** Of course, because the antagonist is more powerful and more prepared than the protagonist, there is no question that the antagonist will win the fight. All the main character's planning and preparation fail. He is defeated — left with no resources except himself alone. It is at this lowest point in the drama that the main character comes face to face with the skeleton of fear, doubt, and faithlessness that has been starved in its locked cell for a lifetime. The Action-Adventure protagonist is no naive romantic, but a character who must confront the terror of the death mask head-on and answer its demand of deed over word. In *The Bridges at Toko-Ri* (script by Valentine Davis), downed Navy Lt. Harry Brubaker (William Holden) and rescue chopper pilot Mike Forney (Mickey Rooney) are surrounded by North Korean troops behind enemy lines. Their chances of remaining alive through the night are nonexistent.

MIKE FORNEY
Do you know how to fire a carbine,
Sir? Just release the safety
there and squeeze the trigger.
Fires automatically.

LT. HARRY BRUBAKER
I'm a lawyer from Denver,
Colorado, Mike. I probably can't
hit a thing.

MIKE FORNEY
Jesus, how'd you get out here in a
smelly ditch in Korea?

ACTION-ADVENTURE STRUCTURE

>   LT. HARRY BRUBAKER
>   That's just what I've been asking
>   myself.

Unlike the self-revelation of other dramas, however, the Action-Adventure character's resolve to act is an acceptance of the near-certain likelihood of death. In the penultimate scenes of *Terminator 2: Judgment Day* (script by James Cameron & William Wisher Jr.), as the T-2, John, and his mother stand on the scaffolding above a boiling cauldron of molten metal, the Terminator has come to recognize that the evil loosed upon the human world is contained within his own makeup. John takes out the only remaining relic of the first Terminator, a metallic hand, and the controlling computer chip, and drops them into the cauldron, where they melt into the slag.

>   SARAH
>   It's finally over.

>   TERMINATOR
>   No. There is another chip.

> The T-2 touches a metal finger to the side
> of his head. With a glance, both he and
> Sarah understand the sacrifice he must make.
> John suddenly understands what he means.

>   TERMINATOR
>   I have to go away, John. It must
>   end here... or I am the future.

                         JOHN
            Don't do it. Please... don't go —

Terminator puts his hand on John's shoulder.
He moves slightly and the human side of his
face comes into the light.

He reaches down toward John's face. His
metal finger touches the tear trickling down
his cheek.

                       TERMINATOR
            I know now why you cry, though it
            is something I can never do.

He turns and steps off the edge.

In some cases it may be acceptance of the death of a portion
of one's soul. In *Shane* (script by A. B. Guthrie), Alan Ladd's
drifter commits to take action on behalf of the farmers
against Jack Palance's sadistic gunfighter, Jack Wilson,
knowing that not only is he risking his life, but relinquishing
any claim he might have on a place in a peaceful society.

                        SHANE
            I gotta be going on.

                        JOEY
         Why, Shane?

```
                    SHANE
        A man has to be what he is, Joey.
        You can't break the mold.  I tried
        it and it didn't work for me.


                    JOEY
        We want you, Shane.


                    SHANE
        Joey, there's no living with a
        killing.  There's no going back
        from one. Right or wrong, it's a
        brand.  A brand that sticks.
        There's no going back.
```

In *Full Metal Jacket*, the conflict of Vietnam becomes Joker's (Mathew Modine) agonizingly personal epitaph to his own illusions when he is forced to administer the *coup de grâce* at close range to a wounded Vietnamese sniper. Joker and the Marine squad have tracked the sniper into the burning lobby of what was once, perhaps, an ornate hotel. He inches slowly into the room, keeping cover behind a marble column until he sees a small, black-clad figure standing at the window. He raises his rifle to fire at the sniper's back, but his gun jams! The sniper whirls around, face-to-face with Joker, the delicate, fine-boned features of a beautiful, teenage Vietnamese girl. Joker frantically works the bolt of his M-16 while slugs from the sniper's AK-47 tear chunks of masonry from the column in front of him. She edges around for a better shot — but suddenly her body explodes from a burst of automatic fire.

Rafterman snaps another M-16 magazine into place, gestures Joker to stay put, then moves to the window and shouts to the two men in the square.

                    RAFTERMAN
          We got the sniper!

The Sniper lies on the floor, writhing in pain.

Joker and Rafterman cautiously approach her. Rafterman kicks away her AK-47.

The two men stare at her in disbelief: The Sniper is a child, no more than fifteen years old, a slender Eurasian angel with dark beautiful eyes.

Animal Mother calls from behind cover at the other end of the room.

                    ANIMAL MOTHER
          Joker?

                    JOKER
          Yo.

                    ANIMAL MOTHER
          What's up?

                    JOKER
          We got the sniper.

Rafterman and Joker circle around the Sniper
as Donlon and T.H.E. Rock and Animal Mother
walk up.

                    RAFTERMAN
          I saved Joker's ass. I got the
          sniper. I fucking blew her away.

Rafterman laughs hysterically, and kisses
his rifle.

                    RAFTERMAN
          Am I bad? Am I a life-taker? Am I
          a heart-breaker?

The Sniper gasps, whimpers. Donlon stares at
her.

                    DONLON
          What's she saying?

                    JOKER
          She's praying.

                    T.H.E. ROCK
          No more boom-boom for this baby-
          san. There's nothing we can do for
          her. She's dead meat.

                    ANIMAL MOTHER
          Okay. Let's get the fuck outta
          here.

                    JOKER
          What about her?

                    ANIMAL MOTHER
          Fuck her. Let her rot.

The Sniper prays in Vietnamese.

                    JOKER
          We can't just leave her here.

                    SNIPER
              (whimpering)
          Sh... sh-shoot... me. Shoot... me.

                    ANIMAL MOTHER
          If you want to waste her, go on,
          waste her.

                    SNIPER
              (gasping)
          Shoot... me... shoot... me.

Joker slowly lifts his pistol and looks into
her eyes.

                    SNIPER
          Shoot... me.

Joker jerks the trigger. BANG!

The four men are silent.

Joker stares down at the dead girl.

                    DONLON
          Hard core, man. Fucking hard core.

- ❏ **COMMITMENT** The external goal is now far more important for both the main character and the antagonist. The antagonist has driven the protagonist into a life-threatening compulsion to support a moral principle. If the main character fails to achieve the goal, a great deal will be lost because the action affects not only the main character but the society that encompasses that value.

  Equally important, the antagonist is likewise committed to achieve a goal that is valued by the opposing society. In *Battle of the Bulge* (script by Bernard Gordon, John Melson, Milton Sperling), Robert Shaw's Panzer tank commander Col. Martin Hessler declares to his shocked corporal why he continues to fight even though it is certain that the German army has lost the war.

                    COL. MARTIN HESSLER
          We have outrun the other Panzers.
          The eyes of Germany are on us. The

Fuhrer himself will decorate me.
We have done it, Conrad. We have
done it.

          CPL. CONRAD
Then I was wrong. We have won the
war.

          COL. MARTIN HESSLER
No.

          CPL. CONRAD
We have lost?

          COL. MARTIN HESSLER
No.

          CPL. CONRAD
I do not understand. We have not
won and we have not lost. What is
happening?

          COL. MARTIN HESSLER
The best thing possible is
happening. The war will go on.

          CPL. CONRAD
For how long?

          COL. MARTIN HESSLER
Indefinitely. On and on and on.

```
          CPL. CONRAD
But it must come to an end.

          COL. MARTIN HESSLER
You are a fool, Conrad.  Those of
us who understood knew in 1941 we
could never win.

          CPL. CONRAD
You mean, Colonel, for three years
we have been fighting without any
hope of victory?

          COL. MARTIN HESSLER
There are many kinds of victory.
For the German army to survive.
For us to remain in uniform. That
is our victory.  Conrad, the world
is not going to get rid of us
after all.
```

❑ **SHOWDOWN** Compromise between the main character and the antagonist is impossible. They must fight. Only one can win. This is the moment of truth that the entire Action-Adventure story has been about, and it is the only way the dramatic conflict can be settled to the audience's *satisfaction*.

❑ **JOIN-UP** In most Action-Adventure stories, the main character will defeat the antagonist and, moreover, will secure a place in society because of the heroic deed. It is not merely coincidental that in *The African Queen*, Charlie Allnut and Rosie get married just before they are to be hanged, or that Juda in *Ben-Hur*, Cameron Poe in *Con Air*, and John McClane in *Die Hard* are returned to their families. They have not only earned their place in the larger society, but also the audience-pleasing satisfaction of *belonging*. Even Gonville Bromhead in *Zulu* surpasses his elite class to join a new family, the company of common men.

Because the audience has invested its emotions and time in wanting the main character to succeed, the viewers will be very unsatisfied if the protagonist dies without accomplishing the goal — unless that death is made worthy by an achievement greater than the original objective. Although in *Braveheart* and *Viva Zapata!* the protagonists are killed, their deaths become more meaningful because they are public executions committed by the hands of deceitful antagonists. The societal consequence of these parables is that the protagonists are beatified beyond human status into saviors with spiritual powers. Their deaths are consecrated, and they are given a patrician's dominion over ordinary mankind.

"THE FUTURE IS JUST ONE DAMNED THING AFTER ANOTHER."

— WINSTON CHURCHILL

Because each particular film genre sets up certain expectations of content and meaning for an audience, the screenwriter needs to know not only how the individual building blocks fit together in a sequence to make a well-structured, coherent plot, but also the overarching impact to be made on the audience from the totality of the component parts. Any given scene arising from one or more structural elements may, by itself, create a memorable impression on the audience. The murder in the shower in Alfred Hitchcock's *Psycho* kept many women from taking showers for years. Likewise, the very palpable torture of Babe (Dustin Hoffman) by the Nazi dentist Szell (Sir Lawrence Olivier) in *Marathon Man* (script by William Goldman) is painful to recall even without watching the film. In some cases, even a line of dialogue can become a catch phrase for an entire movie.

> LT. COL. BILL KILGORE
> I love the smell of napalm in the morning.[4]

> HARRY CALLAHAN
> Go ahead, make my day.[5]

> THE GODFATHER
> I'm gonna make him an offer he can't refuse.[6]

The effectiveness of a good Action-Adventure film must be judged by the overall energy that propels an audience from beginning through the stages of the unfolding story. A good screenwriter must develop an *earned instinct* for where the story needs to go and, like following the arched flight of an arrow, a sense of when the story veers off its path.

[4] John Milius and Francis Ford Coppola, Michael Herr, *Apocalypse Now* (1979).

[5] Joseph Stinson, *Sudden Impact* (1983).

[6] Francis Ford Coppola, Mario Puzo, *The Godfather* (1972).

Narrative Trajectory

The anchor point of the arrow's flight is the archer's bow, and from the angle of this release and our experience of the world, we know more or less where the arrow will land. A screenwriter's earned instinct for the Narrative Trajectory of a story functions in an analogous sense as the dramatic hook gets the story started. The anticipation rises to the height of the complications, and the promise of final resolution inevitably bends the tip earthward. It is the screenwriter's mastery of this overarching Narrative Trajectory that the audience puts their faith in, the curve of the storyteller's line that will carry them safely over make-believe time and space toward ultimate satisfaction.

An Action-Adventure story normally begins with, or very quickly becomes a state of siege, a pressure-cooker standoff and imminent confrontation between the elements of good and evil:

- In *Apocalypse Now*, the rogue U.S. Army Colonel Walter Kurtz (Marlon Brando) has established his own outlaw kingdom upriver in Vietnam. Capt. Benjamin Willard (Martin Sheen) is sent to besiege Kurtz, an Impossible Mission as insane as the siege of Vietnam itself.

- The enigmatic stranger in *Shane* arrives in the society of hardworking frontier farmers who are beset by Jack Wilson's (Jack Palance) ruthless hired guns sent by the cattlemen to intimidate them off their land.

- Will Kane anxiously awaits alone for the arrival of the gunslingers who've sworn vengeance against him at *High*

Noon while the townsfolk barricade themselves in a self-imposed blockade.

- The peasants of the small Mexican village are at the mercy of the marauding bandits who force them into virtual slavery until they are set free by *The Magnificent Seven*.

- *Battleground* and *Battle of the Bulge* depict the Allies dug in against the surprise Nazi onslaught in the Ardennes. *The Dirty Dozen*, *The Guns of Navarone*, and *A Bridge Too Far* lay siege to unassailable German strongholds, and virtually every World War II Action-Adventure film such as *The Longest Day* and *Saving Private Ryan*, is about the siege of the European fortress that the Nazis called *Festung Europa*.

It is, in fact, precisely the pressure of the hot-box siege that ultimately explodes the events of Action-Adventure stories into high-octane action. Ordinarily, a Briefing of minimal back story exposition establishes that all attempts at negotiation, subterfuge, etc. have failed, or are impossible for one reason or another, so that now there is an urgent need for direct physical action in order to break the stalemate. This looming confrontation sets the goal, which, in turn, dictates the degree and type of action required to resolve the impasse. In this way, the breaking point of the tension, like the velocity stored in the archer's straining bow, snaps the physical action of the plot into place, and flings both protagonist and antagonist toward each other on an inescapable collision course. They clash in the story's chase resolution. In Action-Adventure terms, the chase may involve a literal pursuit as the protagonist and antagonist fight for the advantage, but the decisive chase of Action-Adventure is the full-out battle sequence where the two opponents hound each other to the death.

101

Michael Mann's *Heat* sets up a tense state of siege between Robert De Niro's master crook Neil McCauley and Al Pacino's fanatical cop Vincent Hanna as they match strengths until, in the end, the two of them perform a treacherous slow-motion chase to the death. At one point, the adversaries, crook and cop, actually sit down across from each other in a restaurant, to have coffee like normal men amid a swirl of normal people. But these are not normal men. They are men for whom violence is a daily occupation, and who unequivocally declare their resolve to maintain those occupations.

                    NEIL
          This regular-type life. That your
          life?

                    VINCENT
          My life. No, my life? No, my
          life's a disaster zone. I've got
          a stepdaughter so fucked up
          because her real father's this
          large-type asshole. I got a wife.
          We're passing each other on the
          downslope of a marriage. My
          third. Because I spend all my
          time chasing guys like you around
          the block. That's my life.

                    NEIL
          Guy told me one time. Don't let
          yourself get attached to anything

you are not willing to walk out on
in thirty seconds flat if you feel
the heat around the corner. Now,
if you're around me and you've got
to move when I move, how do you
expect to keep a marriage?

                VINCENT
That's an interesting point. What
are you, a monk?

                NEIL
I have a woman.

                VINCENT
What do you tell her?

                NEIL
I tell her I'm a salesman.

                VINCENT
So then, if you spot me coming
around that corner, you just going
to walk out on this woman?

                NEIL
I'd say good-bye. That's the
discipline.

                VINCENT
That's pretty vague.

```
                    NEIL
     It is what it is.   It's that or we
     both got to go do something else,
     pal.


                  VINCENT
     I don't know how to do anything
     else.


                    NEIL
     Neither do I.


                  VINCENT
     I don't much want to, either.


                    NEIL
     Neither do I.
```

In most Action-Adventure stories, the siege breaks out in the second or third act, to become the action-chase sequence that forces the protagonist and antagonist to come face to face in a Showdown. In contrast, most Thriller films tend to be driven initially by a pursuit that inexorably tightens focus on the threat, and limits the physical space until the final defensive siege, when the cornered protagonist ultimately stands on ground stripped of all defenses.

The essential Narrative Trajectory is a characteristic outgrowth of the Initial Contact, that distinctive inciting incident that hooks the audience into watching the story. What's going to happen? How are they going to get out of this situation? If the Initial Contact starts, for instance, as an unexplained attempt on the main character's life in a Thriller, then the character's natural reaction is fear, confusion, panic, and the impulse to run, which immediately sets the Narrative Trajectory as a chase. Roger Thornhill (Cary Grant in *North by Northwest*) is mistaken for a government agent by a group of spies who intend to kill him. With absolutely no idea initially of why he is a target for death, and cut off from anyone who might believe the threat against him, including the police, Thornhill takes the rational action that any normal person would take — he *runs away* to save his life. But the conspirators are determined to find him, and there's no way Thornhill can run far enough or fast enough, so he must ultimately turn the tables by placing the spies under siege.

In *Three Days of the Condor*, Robert Redford's Joe Turner is a low-level CIA employee who returns to work after lunch to discover that everyone in his office has been brutally murdered. There's no time to wait around and figure things out. Turner runs to escape the same fate. Later, his tactics turn to forcing the hand of the stonewalled CIA operatives through an intellectual hide-and-seek that exposes their malevolent conspiracy.

On the other hand, if the main character and the surrounding society are, or soon will be, vulnerable to the siege of a superior antagonist, then the agonizing pressure requires a build-up of stamina, or the gathering of reinforcements, until enough explosive power can be summoned to rupture the blockage.

In *Die Hard* and *Die Hard: With a Vengeance*, Det. John McClane is the only defender that stands between a beleaguered society and the offensive of a supremely sophisticated army of criminals. First, McClane must thwart the force, then turn the tables by going on the attack himself.

The Alamo, *55 Days at Peking*, *Zulu*, and hundreds of other Action-Adventure films present characters who are literally under siege inside walled fortresses, while *The Guns of Navarone*, *The Dirty Dozen*, and others present characters who must assault highly defended fortifications to achieve the Impossible Mission. More often than not, after the tension of a lengthy preparation, the assault breaks out into hot pursuit followed by hand-to-hand fighting to secure the objective.

If the screenwriter doesn't keep an eye firmly fixed on the guiding arrow of Narrative Trajectory, there will inevitably be unsatisfied audience members. They may not be able to articulate their frustration, and may even struggle to declare certain sections of a film as particularly expressive; but because, on the whole, the Narrative Trajectory is out of equilibrium they will have missed that sense of completion a good story must have.

For all that was admirable in the factual accuracy of both *Wyatt Earp* and *Tombstone*, each film failed to adhere to a secure trajectory. The central dramatic conflict in the two films is the historical gunfight at the O.K. Corral between the Earps and the Clantons. As often as not, however, no matter how remarkable the separate events of any historical episode may be, taken all together they do not make for a good dramatic story. In terms of portraying the reality of place, era, and event, both of these films are far more historically correct than 1959s box-office hit *Gunfight at the O.K. Corral.* In striving for period accuracy, however, both films skewed the Narrative Trajectory off course. Neither builds to the culminating event of the famous gunfight as the Showdown resolution of a *dramatic* conflict between the sides. Instead, each cinematic version of the Earp legend uses that episode as nothing more than an undifferentiated event in a string of life events, with the result that there is no rising tension and no sense of a satisfying sweep to the stories.

Likewise, in *Three Kings*, not only do the protagonists meander off-course from their questionable mission, but the Narrative Trajectory is constantly, irritatingly interrupted by events and characters that have nothing whatsoever to do with the story. The audience is continually sidetracked by the antics of a clueless reporter, harangued by long chunks of political diatribe, and completely kicked out of the story by the excesses of slow-motion bullet effects that more properly belong in a computer game.

Graham Yost, the screenwriter of *Speed* has declared: "I think once we got on the bus, we should have stayed on the bus. I think the subway sequence had some pluses for it, but it felt like a repeat. The movie feels like it's over when they come out from underneath the bus. That's the emotional high point of the movie."[7] What Graham Yost is talking about is the Narrative Trajectory of the movie.

---

[7] "Action! An Interview With Graham Yost," by David Konow. *Creative Screenwriting*, Vol. 8. No. 2, 2001.

Scribble Exercise:

❏ What was the most significant event to occur in your life during the past three days? A new job? Finding a lost sock? A new love? A rescued puppy? Discovering a secret restaurant? Write a letter to your best friend describing *only* those actions from the past three days that *directly*, unswervingly led up to your significant event.

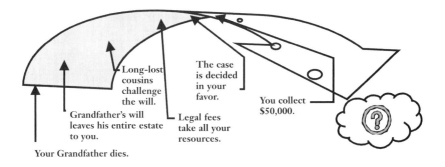

Long-lost cousins challenge the will.

The case is decided in your favor.

You collect $50,000.

Grandfather's will leaves his entire estate to you.

Legal fees take all your resources.

Your Grandfather dies.

❏ Draw a diagram of the Narrative Trajectory for your own life from one year ago until one year from now.

• Choose an anchor point, the beginning of your personal drama, that has set you on a specific course with an anticipated end.

• Plot the specific events that define the path of your drama.

- What was or will be the apex of the flight curve, the highest point of greatest conflict, tension, or risk?

- Where do you anticipate the trajectory of your arrow will descend to earth in twelve more months, i.e., how will your personal drama come to a definitive end?

- What evidence will you have that your drama has come to a marked conclusion of events that began one year ago?

- If an audience were watching this story as a film, would the viewers know that it is finished? Would they be satisfied with the conclusion?

CHAPTER 6

THE ACTION! OF ACTION-ADVENTURE

In every cliché sketch of a silent movie set, the archetypical director slaps a riding crop against his puttees and yells, "Action!" while the cinematographer furiously hand-cranks a giant tripod-mounted camera. This scene has become such an everyday image in our popular consciousness that even the word *action* uttered in certain circumstances can get a laugh. In the screenwriting business, the term *action* is used so loosely that there is very little distinction, much less consistent example, by which to understand its meaning. The one thing that it should *not* signify is that simply because a film contains mashed metal, that automatically makes it an Action-Adventure movie. The smash-and-crash sort of action can occur in a Thriller, a Detective film, or even a Comedic Drama. The fact is, *action* exists on several different levels and has a number of different senses depending on the application, so we need to establish the semantic territory.

IS SOMETHING GOING TO HAPPEN? — ACTION AS DECISION

At the most fundamental level, *dramatic action* is not the physical exploit that we ordinarily think of as characterizing Action-Adventure films, but the *decision process* that precedes the physical action and makes it unavoidable.

Characters in a drama, exactly like people in everyday life, continually make choices, from the trivial to the crucial, based on their best guess of how those choices will influence their lives. You may choose to go see a particular movie, take out a loan to buy a car, get married, or refuse to help a friend because, either instinctively or after long consideration, you've weighed the odds on how your decision will change your life. Obviously, the more financial risk, personal Commitment, or time and energy it costs, the more you will normally dwell on the decision. In this way, most of us manage to negotiate our way through life without too many shocking surprises. We've prepared for the future by making choices we believe will yield favorable outcomes. Of course, we know we may not always guess right, so we usually take only the minimum action necessary to achieve what we want. We rarely ever take a truly big risk, not merely because such a risk would put our finances, domestic happiness, or even freedom in jeopardy, but because taking such a gigantic leap of faith would endanger our very concept of who we are. Guessing wrong would mean that we would have to readjust our carefully protected self-image, and most of us will do virtually *anything* to avoid that threat.

But drama is not real life. Drama is life condensed to its essential elements and encapsulated. The screenwriter constructs situations for a dramatic character in which the decision has a momentous consequence. But the choice will not produce the expected results for the character or the audience, and that unanticipated result will force the character to make yet another difficult decision, which will also not produce the predicted result, and so forth, until the conflict between the main character and the antagonist reaches a point where the main character *must* come to grips with self-concept in order to resolve the external problem in a decisive way. Put simply, it is the hard choices a character must make that are the dramatic action of the story. Without this dramatic action in which difficult decisions are made, there is absolutely no motivation for the characters to engage in physical action. This fact is an indispensable foundation that lesser Action-Adventure movies frequently fail to recognize when the writer shoves the characters into non-stop action for no legitimate reason. A mere list of stunts, no matter how inventive or how engaging each may be, is not dramatic in the least — because the actions are not performed in the service of a decision. *Nothing happens.*

NOTHING HAPPENS — DECOMPOSITION WITHOUT ACTION

On the extreme left flank of the Genre Continuum, Private Anguish is the most static, action-less, form of drama. This is a genre that is relatively unusual in American film, but frequently occurs in European cinema. For the most part it is a highly literary form of character investigation. Like a novel, the Private Anguish film attempts to expose the interior thoughts and feelings of a character. For the most part, however, because the characters are consumed with themselves and are not actually doing anything, these films must resort to rather strained visual symbolism. They use lingering shots of a bleak external landscape, for instance, to represent the equally austere and depressing inner life of the character. Mirrors, windows, and water reflect prominently the character's brooding face, and the literary technique of a voiceover narrative is often used to illuminate the character's thoughts. Some of the world's most honored filmmakers such as Ingmar Bergman have made the Private Anguish film almost a signature genre. Using the stunning visuals of his cinematographer Sven Nyquist, Bergman has created such memorable films in the genre as *Persona* and *Cries and Whispers*. However, despite all their somber grace, these movies are almost literally without movement; for our purposes, there is no "action." *Nothing happens.*

SOMETHING OUGHT TO HAPPEN — CONFLICT WITHOUT ACTION

More common in American films is the Pivotal Conflict drama. Typically, a Pivotal Conflict movie is essentially a one-room stage play that has been transliterated to film. Movies as diverse as *Driving Miss Daisy*, *A Simple Plan*, *Marvin's Room*, and *Prince of Tides* are Pivotal Conflict dramas. The source material for each of these movies is either a stage play or a novel, and each carries the inbuilt structure of its parent medium. They are only a half-step removed from the Private Anguish dramas. Instead of bounding the drama inside the mind of a character, the Pivotal Conflict drama is bounded inside the physical limitations of a house or other confining structure, which forces the characters to be in uncomfortable proximity to each other. Even though the movie versions of these dramas attempt to breathe "air" into these productions contriving excuses for outside locations, there is truly no compelling Narrative Trajectory to command expansion beyond the one-room situation for which they were originally designed.   In fact, relieving the restricted setting actually weakens the impact that the pressure of confinement has on the characters.

SOMETHING HAPPENS — ACTION AS MOVEMENT

It's not for nothing that the caricature silent-film director hollers "Action!" In the first place, he is commanding the actors to *act*, that is, to stop being themselves, get into the roles of their characters and make believe the drama. As self-evident as this may seem, it is actually an extremely delicate, exacting, and emotionally demanding task for which actors train and condition themselves. At that instant, they must, whatever their particular philosophy of acting may be, transform themselves into the character that the writer has written on the page. It is here that the screenwriter must take enormous care in providing the actors with enough cues on the page so that they have access not only to the obvious, external nature of the characters, but to their internal workings as well.

In the second instance, "Action!" commands the actors to move about, not aimlessly wander from one piece of furniture to another on the set, but to move with purpose and direction. At sometime in the rehearsal period, the director and the actors have worked out each of these actions, and the director has blocked the scene to coordinate the motions of the actors with the changes in direction or the lens settings of the camera. It is a complex ballet of muscle and technology, emotion and mechanism, that will ultimately register a sense of dramatic propulsion on film.

But where do the actors and director get their *actions*? From the script. If the writer doesn't put the words on the page, the actors can't put them in their mouths. However, no experienced screenwriter ever literally describes the movements an actor must make. There would be nothing more boring in a script than to write, "George takes six steps from the sofa to the bar. He reaches for the bottle of scotch with his right hand. His left hand takes a glass from the shelf." Besides, no actor would pay any attention to those literal stage directions because there is no way the screenwriter can know what the actual shooting circumstances will be. Perhaps the scene must be shot on the beach instead of the living room, in which case the instruction to walk to the bar is nonsensical. The screenwriter's craft is not to describe action on the screen with such exactitude, but to provide an impetus for the movement. Give the actors the tools, but don't tell them how to do their job. "George clenches at the Scotch. The rim of the glass surrenders to a shrill whine as he grabs the trembling bottle."

SOMETHING'S GOTTA HAPPEN — ACTION AS PLOT

It is in the requirement of *action as plot* that the Action-Adventure genre is most misunderstood, and where a great many lower-budget and foreign attempts at the genre fail. Action as physical pyrotechnics on the screen is not enough to make a movie. Physical action, i.e., stunts, car chases, falls, etc., are, by themselves, completely meaningless. They are a filmed circus, possibly admirable for the skills involved or even for the imaginative cinematography and editing, but unless they are performed for the advancement of the story, they are useless exercises in wasting money and screen time. A number of young European admirers of American Action-Adventure have attempted to imitate the genre. Of course, they have nowhere near the massive budgets of a Hollywood studio picture; but truly good Action-Adventure does not really depend on the size or expense of the action stunts involved. Instead, these ambitious filmmakers use what they have at hand: cars, guns, natural terrain, and limitless enthusiasm. Unfortunately, many of them see in the Hollywood pictures only the overpowering visuals, and understandably mistake those elements for the sole ingredients for Action-Adventure.

Even some films that come in the guise of American Action-Adventure productions plainly miss the essence of the underlying mythology that drives an Action-Adventure film: an organic foundation which requires the action to be the outgrowth of thorny moral dilemmas.

Enemy at the Gates is a visually astonishing account of the World War II siege of Stalingrad. The opening scenes are the most gut-wrenchingly close renderings of the war's imminent death that one can experience in a movie theater. For many people in the audience, the film is surely the first awareness they have had of the consummate brutality and unthinkable human slaughter of that savage campaign. And yet, for all the potential of the powerful opening imagery, the film never progresses beyond its initial impact because, unlike the best of Action-Adventure films, it never challenges its characters (with one exception) to make tough *moral* decisions about their actions. The result is that the action, although it is historically accurate, becomes repetitive, tedious, predictable, and, at times, even outright boring. Vasilli Zaigtsev, the rustic young man who becomes a rallying point for the besieged Red Army because of his expert marksmanship as a sniper, simply goes out each day to kill German officers, returning each evening with a tabulation. It is a job; a better job than the bloodbath of canon fodder that awaits his comrades, but nevertheless a job of calculated, nearly ritual formality. Even the deaths of close associates seem to have no effect on Vasilli. Despite an early scene showing Vasilli's hesitation to kill as a boy, he never questions what he does or why, and only at one point does he even attempt to describe the sniper's unique posture of communion with the human being he is about to exterminate. However, even this pale account lacks any insight or self-revelation, and has no impact whatsoever on the actions Vasilli takes. From the standpoint of the main character who is dramatically responsible for carrying the story, the actions of the plot do not progress or escalate one whit from the beginning of the film to the end. There is no Narrative Trajectory at all. Again, nothing happens.

The fact is that on-screen big-action exhibitions (known as "set pieces") of vehicle chases, gun battles, fist fights, explosions, etc., when we can now use the term *action*, are *dramatically static*. No matter how many characters are dismembered, demolished, or deceased in these sequences, from a dramatic point of view, nothing happens. Unless the motivation for these actions is known, and the outcome results in unforeseen changes, the progress of the story will not intensify. The plot doesn't *move* unless something happens.

"What is written without effort is in general read without pleasure."

— Dr. Samuel Johnson, 1709 – 1784

Everything in a drama is active through cause-and-effect plausibility. The physical actions of the characters are driven by their obsession to reach the exterior goal. Whether their physical actions are successful or not depends on the difficult choices those characters make — and the choices are driven, in turn, by the character's self-concept as shaped by an inner need.

Imagine a simple scene with two characters, George and Martha, on a survival trek through the jungle. George spots a vine dangling over a small, slime-covered pond in the middle of the path. On impulse, he uses the vine to swing over the putrid puddle to the far side. Impressed with himself, he swings back, gathers Martha in his arms, and once more lofts across the sink hole. This time, however, their combined weight breaks the vine, and the two of them plunge into the fetid water. What happened in the story? Nothing. The audience members may laugh at George's misfortune, or they may see the gag coming and merely endure the stunt, hoping for some surprise. They may or may not learn something about George's character.

They certainly know next to zero about Martha's character. But, most important, George's antics have done absolutely nothing to advance the plot, whatever it may be. The viewers are left to surmise what his motivation for the awkward frolic might have been; and in the absence of any evidence to the contrary, they're most likely to assume that George is nothing more than a rather childish, self-indulgent character who is not even worthy of the significance of the survival drama in which he's been placed.

The original *Lethal Weapon* contains a scene that is functionally just as frivolous as George's jungle gymnastics. Det. Riggs (Mel Gibson) and Sgt. Murtaugh (Danny Glover) are sidetracked by rescue operations for a potential suicide jumper. With no motivation to get involved, much less any responsibility, Riggs scampers out onto the ledge and, while babbling that he's equally suicidal, handcuffs himself to the jumper, then leaps from the building, tugging the terrified man after him. Of course, what the suicide has not seen — and neither has the audience — is the giant air bag that has been inflated on the ground. The worst cheat of this completely useless scene is not the hoax put over on the jumper, but the shameless con pulled on the audience. Neither the story nor the character is advanced in any manner whatsoever by this gratuitous fluff. Once again, *nothing happens.*

In *Sleepy Hollow*, Constable Ichabod Crane and the Headless Horseman engage in an extravagant battle inside a windmill, until Crane and his companions barely escape the supernatural top-lopper. But even as they are running away, they observe aloud what the audience has long since been scratching its collective noggin about. If the Horseman is a ghostlike immortal who cannot be killed, why did Crane bother to lure him into the windmill brawl in the first place? Very good question. The only answer is that the scene occurs purely and simply as an audience bamboozle, a prime case of conspicuous disdain on the part of the filmmakers, who tried to hoodwink us into ignoring that there is no motivation for this non-action. Nothing happens.

SOMETHING GOD HATH WROUGHT — *GRAND GUIGNOL* ACTION

What do *Volcano*, *Twister*, *Earthquake*, *The Poseidon Adventure*, *Towering Inferno*, and *Godzilla* have in common? They are all members of a special sub-set of Action-Adventure films: *Don't — Mess — With — Mother — Nature!* In some respects they fulfill the requirements of Action-Adventure, inasmuch as the central cause-and-effect event forces the characters to take action — to save their lives, civilization, or the world — but the fact is that tornadoes, earthquakes, fires, great ocean waves, and even outsized mutated creatures do not have a conscious agenda for destruction. That is, these forces of Mother Nature are just doing what they do — spewing out lava, ripping up ground, or sloshing big ships upside down, without any antagonistic intent. They exist literally on a different timescale from the human characters in the drama, and have no knowledge of or concern for the effects they have on the populated world. The fundamental question raised by the Narrative Trajectory, then, is boringly elemental: Will the human characters survive or not? Ho hum, call us when you know the answer. The characters are not forced to make decisions other than those necessary for pure survival, a sort of intellectual roulette.

The real drama in these disaster films comes from the conflict among the characters themselves. The giant tornado in *Twister* couldn't care less how many cows, trucks or Kansas farm girls it sucks into its vortex. It is completely amoral. But the characters of Bill and Jo Harding (Bill Paxton and Helen Hunt) are vitally concerned with the restoration of their relationship. While all the hullabaloo of twister chasing is going on, what's really at stake is the future happiness of this couple — and the audience very much wants to see them get back together.

It is absolutely essential in these hell-and-high-water survival epics that the dramatic action stem, not from the ordeals of the external whiz-bang special effects circumstances, but from the very difficult emotional and moral choices the characters are forced to make *about their relationships to each other* because of the time pressure of imminent annihilation.

SOMETHING IS DEFINITELY HAPPENING — ACTION AS SKID-'N-SCREECH OPERA

Currently, the undisputed masters of slam-bang Action-Adventure are Jerry Bruckheimer and Joel Silver. Between the two of them, they have produced such box-office mega-hits as *The Rock*, *Armageddon*, *Con Air*, and *Swordfish*. Bruckheimer and Silver are, in many ways, the logical inheritors of the long-standing cinematic tradition begun by early filmmakers like Mack Sennett and D. W. Griffith. Their films use the loudest, fastest, highest, and most stupendous special effects and action stunts put on screen and, in the best of the Action-Adventure tradition, their best works such as *Con Air* also adhere to the morality-play origins of the genre. Hollywood has always banked on the extravagant, the extraordinary, the faster, and the larger-than-life — in everything from the Keystone Kops to the disaster epics of Irwin Allen's *Towering Inferno* and *Poseidon Adventure*. In 1927s *The General*, Buster Keaton actually wrecked a real-life, full-sized train, not to mention countless outbuildings and railroad cars. What is generally regarded as the very first narrative film ever produced, Georges Méliès' 1902 *A Trip To The Moon*, is a special-effects festival produced on an outdoor stage by hand-cranking the film backward in the camera for double-exposure shots.

However, screenwriters should keep in mind that trying to top the newest, hottest, and costliest sensation is not essential to creating a good Action-Adventure screenplay. Production budgets may rise or fall, special-effects scenes come and go, but the fundamental Action-Adventure *story* is still the underpinning of a good film. It is a mistake to place your bets on squeal and sparkle to the sacrifice of a good story. For an Action-Adventure film to work, the story should be solidly riveted to the mythic foundation underlying all enduring classic Action-Adventure films.

How Do We Know Something's Happening? — Action on the Page

In spite of the stale axiom, "the script is the blueprint," a screenplay is far more encompassing than any mere diagram. If the adage were true, screenwriters could merely list a shorthand summary of scenes with sketchy dialogue.

```
INT.   THE BOWLING ALLEY

George and Martha bowl.

                    GEORGE
          (He says something to Martha about
          wanting to go home.)

George rolls a ball.  The pins explode.  The
bowling alley burns down.
```

No doubt a good director can take this lifeless fragment and devise special effects, stunt action, and even characters from this negligible substance. Truly inventive actors can even flesh out their characters with imaginary lives. However, nothing the director and actors accomplish will be the product of the writer's contribution to the film. The writer's creative spirit will not infuse the picture in the slightest. The scene might as well have been upchucked by a word processor, as some "dramatic creation" computer programs profess to do. Regrettably, this sort of dreary, jaded prose is not as uncommon as you might imagine.

The objective of a good screenplay is to give the reader a distinctive, engaging experience. Ideally, the reader is so caught up in the pages that there is no conscious awareness of reading a screenplay. *Screenwriting 101* covers screenplay style and format in detail, but a few reminders may be helpful.

1. Do not clutter your presentation with useless abbreviations, numbers, and other indications that have nothing to do with telling the story. Whenever you're tempted to add some adornment such as a shot direction, ask yourself if the decoration kicks the readers out of the story by reminding them that they're reading a screenplay.

2. Make the script easy to read! Use plenty of white space so that the reader can smoothly romp through the script as if the movie were playing out on the pages.

3. Pay close attention to spelling and grammar. Yes, your English teachers were right. The care you take with the formality of language is an indication of the care you take with your overall scriptcraft. Professionals in every field use their best tools to do their work. You owe the reader no less than your meticulous adherence to accepted standards.

4.   For as long as there have been typewriters, the movie and broadcasting industries have used Courier as the standard typeface for script format. Each letter in Courier 12 font (Courier 10 typewriter pitch) takes up exactly the same amount of space regardless of its individual shape. Each page of script in Courier 12 font contains more or less the same number of words that, we know through experience, will equal about one minute of screen time. However, with the advent of the proportionately spaced computer typestyles where each letter takes up only as much room as it needs, words set in Times Roman 12 font, for instance, are squeezed together more (kerned) than Courier 12. The result is that there will be more words to a page, therefore fewer pages to the finished screenplay, and no conventional way to estimate how many actual minutes of screen time each page might represent. Inexperienced script readers who simply glance at the final page number to determine the length of the script base their judgments solely on the quantity of pages without understanding that the typeface used in the script can produce as much as *ten* pages difference in length. More important, to the *experienced* eye, a script in anything *other* than Courier 12 font simply looks *wrong*, because proportionately spaced type crowds the page, making it more difficult to use white space to convey a rhythm to the reader's eye. Therefore, regardless of all the snazzy typestyles available with today's computer programs, Courier 12 font remains the universally followed industry standard for feature film scripts.

ALL YE KNOW ABOUT FILM SCRIPT FORMAT, AND ALL YE NEED TO KNOW.

- Left margin: 1.5 inches

- Right margin: 1.25 inches

- Top & bottom margins: 1 inch

- Tabs: starting from the "0" mark:
  Dialogue: 2.60 inches
  Parentheticals: 3.25 inches
  Character names: 4.0 inches
  Transitions (DISSOLVE TO:): 7.0 inches, flush right

Scribble Exercise:

❑ **At midnight you are just getting into your car in a small shopping center when you suddenly hear someone yell frantically, "Stop! Thief!" You look up to see two men running from a delicatessen. The man being chased is within three feet of you. You are the only person in the parking lot who can stop him from escaping to freedom across the nearby highway. What decision do you make? Why?**

❑ **What are the direct, immediate consequences of your decision? What happens as a result of your decision that you did not expect to happen? For instance:**

- You decide not to act. The thief pulls a gun and kills the delicatessen owner.

- You decide not to act. The delicatessen owner draws a gun and kills the thief. You later discover that the dead man was not a thief at all, but merely in the wrong place at the wrong time.

- You decide to tackle the thief. He pleads with you to let him go free, but you hang on. The pursuer arrives, shoots the man dead, then disappears across the highway never to be seen again.

- You decide to tackle the thief. He swears revenge on you. You discover later that the thief is a member of a particularly vicious gang that is notorious for exacting unspeakable reprisals against anyone who crosses them.

❏ **Your decision and the resulting consequences inescapably affect the way you think about yourself. How must you readjust your self-concept to account for the consequences of your decision to act or not to act?**

CHAPTER SEVEN

ACTION-ADVENTURE CHARACTERS

THE GUY IN THE WHITE HAT

Emerging from dime novels, the Western hero arrived on the frontier of the silver screen early in the development of motion pictures. Tom Mix, William S. Hart, "Bronco Billy" Anderson, and Hopalong Cassidy were genuine white-hat heroes starring in American morality plays that depicted a society of traditional values and definite standards of right and wrong. After all, how can you stand up and cheer for an *Eastern* frontier hero named Natty Bumpo? Nevertheless, although the dime novels themselves had frequently contrived heroes from outlaws, frontiersmen, and even Native Americans, movie audiences couldn't get their fill of the romance and gunplay of the open-range cowboy, a man who always knew right from wrong and was ready to back up his convictions with flying fists and a fast draw on his six-shooter. He was absolutely perfect, untouchable (even virgin), and an unrepentant stranger with no entanglements to confuse his moral charter. For a society thoroughly dazed by the cultural body-blows of World War I, in the midst of whiplashing itself out of the latter stages of Victorian restraint into the recklessness of the twenties, the white-hat cowboy was God's own ordained champion of normalcy.

With the passage of World War II, Action-Adventure developed a somewhat more sophisticated main character in more complex story lines with less well-defined issues of good and bad. The American myth was taking a beating due to the increasingly knotty developments in the geopolitical arena. But at heart, the cagey, grown-up, urban Action-Adventure protagonist is still the same ingenuous adolescent from the flickering black-and-white screen of the Saturday matinee morality plays.

Action-Adventure films are always about an imminent threat to society — the clapboard Western town run riot by lawless gunslingers, New York doomed by a mad bomber, democratic freedom under assault by a megalomaniacal dictator, or the enslavement of a planetary system long ago and far away. Regardless of the scale of the endangered society, the antagonist has manipulated events so that a rapid and forceful response is required by the protagonist.

THE ACTION-ADVENTURE PROTAGONIST:

✓ **IS A LARGER-THAN-LIFE CHARACTER.** The issue of greatness inborn or greatness thrust upon a character may be an element of a particular Action-Adventure story, but in either case, the protagonist is, or becomes, an extraordinary figure. The character may have relatively humble origins, such as William Wallace in *Braveheart* or Emiliano Zapata in

Viva Zapata!, but historic events call upon the character's native capacity for excellence in the selfless service of society. Conversely, the character may be born to a greatness that must yet be proven in battle. Obviously, even within this broad assortment of rank, there is a range of diversity, from Superman to Will Kane, King Henry V to John McClane. The quality of the individual character's greatness, natural or achieved, is an outgrowth of the narrative context, which we will examine later.

✓ **POSSESSES MARTIAL SKILLS AND STRATEGIC RESOURCES.** Action-Adventure is necessarily about physical action. Physical force is absolutely required to break the stalemate of siege and to defeat the antagonist, so the protagonist must be a character who is skilled to some degree in combat. No average dentist, schoolteacher, or writer is capable of taking on the challenge. In fact, average characters of any sort are excluded from leadership in Action-Adventure for the very fact that they do not and cannot possess the requisite martial skills. Imagine if, in the same circumstances of the original *Die Hard*, the character of John McClane were an elementary school textbook salesman visiting his estranged wife. McClane's role in preventing the takeover of the Nakatomi building would be vastly different without his ability to call on the training, skills, and mind-set of a police officer.

✓ **HAS THE AUTHORITY TO CARRY OUT THE MISSION.** Action-Adventure central characters, as a rule, are law enforcement officers or military personnel in some way. It is essential that the character at least be deputized off the record to act on behalf of a lawfully constituted body. Indiana Jones, for instance, is neither a police nor military officer, but he does act on official behalf of the United States government. This authoritative warrant allows the character to bypass and cut through street-level impediments (just think of the cop pursuing the bad guy while holding his gun in one hand and his badge in the other), but more important, it provides the character with the dispensation to take lethal action. It's not only Agent 007 who needs a license to kill, but all Action-Adventure heroes, because they serve to restore social order.

Official ordination may not always be possible, of course. Shane, for instance, acts in a lawless land where no true legal authority exists. The deputization comes not from some on-screen source, but from the audience itself. The protagonist on the screen acts not only on behalf of the society on screen, but for the society in the theater watching the screen; and even the spontaneous dispatch of bad guys can be approved only as an act authorized by the power of the audience. Without both a justifiable reason to act, and a cause that is worthy of their endorsement, the larger society of the theater audience members will refuse to deputize the hero, and the protagonist truly becomes a selfish, vengeful pariah.

✓ **HAS THE MORAL RESPONSIBILITY TO ACT.** Because Action-Adventure stories are morality plays, they are not dispassionate executions of predetermined justice. The main character is allowed to brood over the obligation to do the job, or the methods by which the job must be accomplished, or even the worthiness of the mission, but the conclusive act will be to *do the right thing* because it is the *right thing to do*. As a matter of fact, in the quintessential Action-Adventure film *The Guns of Navarone*, Capt. Keith Mallory (Gregory Peck) and his team of experts secretly assault a massive Nazi gun emplacement on an occupied Greek island. However, almost from the beginning, the righteousness of Mallory's leadership is questioned by two of his specialists who represent opposite moral views of the war. Anthony Quinn's Andrea Stavros is an uncompromising foe of the enemy that killed his wife and children. On the other side, the explosives expert Corp. Miller (David Niven), is an unwilling recruit to the cause.

                    CORPORAL MILLER
          Well, right now I say to hell with
          the job! I've been on a hundred
          jobs and not one of them's altered
          the course of the war!

Mallory bears the moral indictments of both men, both halves of his own conscience, but he ultimately employs all the stealth, force, deceit, and personal risk in his control to accomplish a mission that he is convinced will save the lives of thousands of British troops.

✓ **HAS A PERSONAL CODE OF HONOR.** The main character in an Action-Adventure drama possesses a self-contained code of behavior, a kind of personal nobility that merges with the abstract values of the society under siege. In fact, the hero's code, frequently hard-won through experience, may be much more rigorous than the expedient principles of the world at large, and serves, therefore, to set the hero apart. The hero's personal code of honor distinguishes the hero even more than does a knack for anti-social skills. This curious dichotomy of the professional holding higher standards than the client echoes a deep-seated component of the American chronicle that predates even the myth-making Old West — that we, *by virtue* of our virtue, are stronger, more resolute, and closer to God than the dithering aristocracy of moral wastrels we jettisoned in our Revolution. *Our angels sit more on the right side of heaven than yours do!* Even when our self-less good guys are the bastard children of a foreign creator, they act with more explicit, selfless motivations than do the legitimate heirs. *The Magnificent Seven*, the American adaptation of Akira Kurosawa's Japanese classic *Shichinin No Samurai* (*Seven Samurai*), tells the fable of a loose-knit band of jobless gunslingers who take on the demeaning occupation of saving a Mexican peasant village from the repeated marauding of Eli Wallach's Calvera and his bandits. The indifferent heroes' first try ends shamefully, and they straggle off with their tails dragging behind their kicked butts. But after grumbling that the job isn't worth the peasants' pittance payment, the out-of-work champions finally come to grips with what really sticks in their craw. There is a code of honor among these men, a bond that not only holds them together as matched professionals, but it is stronger than the customs of ordinary mortals, and compels them to put their lives at risk to free the besieged village. In both *Con Air* and

High Noon, the protagonists Cameron Poe and Will Kane deliberately put themselves in harm's way because of a deep Commitment that the code of honor must be upheld regardless of the personal cost.

✓ **HAS FULL GRASP OF THE REQUIRED ACTIONS.** The Action-Adventure protagonist knows that the inevitable result of the decision to act will be a physical fight of lethal proportions. There is no expectation that somehow the problem can be negotiated away, or, for that matter, that rescue in the form of greater or more powerful allies will relieve the responsibility of taking up the fight to its fullest. There may be some fading anticipation of relief, particularly in military situations such as *The Alamo*, *Zulu*, or *Battleground*, but the characters are fully aware that the only realistic alternatives are triumph or death. The deranged parson Rev. Otto Witt escapes from Rourkes Drift only moments before the attack in *Zulu*, screaming a frantic prophecy at the handful of British troops who are about to face ten thousand warriors.

> REV. OTTO WITT
> You're all going to die. Don't
> you realize? Can't you see?
> You're all going to die. Die!
> Death awaits you all.

> PRIVATE THOMAS
> He's right. Why is it us? Why us?

137

> COLOUR SERGEANT BOURNE
> Because we're 'ere, Lad. Nobody
> else. Just us.

✓ **REMAINS FREE OF EMOTIONAL ENTANGLEMENTS.** Blessed cowboys, ever virgin, the early Western movie heroes loved only their horses and politely abstained from the romantic snares of female familiarity. Of course, this anchorite lifestyle kept them free to roam the plains, knights-errant in search of valorous deeds to perform, which is hardly an attribute unique to the American mythos. However, as the genre urbanized away from its pastoral beginnings, the novice loner protagonist grew up to become the Action-Adventure film's don't-give-a-damn, aggressively anti-social, misfit son of a bitch, like Det. Harry Callahan in *Dirty Harry* (script by Dean Riesner).

> HARRY CALLAHAN
> Well, when an adult male is
> chasing a female with intent to
> commit rape, I shoot the bastard.
> That's my policy.

> MAYOR
> Intent? How did you establish
> intent?

> HARRY CALLAHAN
> When a man is chasing a woman
> through an alley with a butcher's

> knife and a hard-on, I figure he
> isn't out collecting for the Red
> Cross.

There's a long catalog of cantankerous troublemakers in the annals of Action-Adventure, from Charlie Allnut, Humphrey Bogart's indifferent river rascal in *The African Queen*, to Mel Gibson's self-destructive Martin Riggs in *Lethal Weapon*. The character of the outsider is not merely a holdover from legendary Western European wanderers like Lancelot, however. The American Action-Adventure protagonist has been barred not only from the larger community, but from family as well. The perpetual conundrum for the genre's leading character is how to preserve the sinuous instincts of the hunter-killer while exposing the naked underbelly of an inner longing for vulnerability.

> VINCENT HANNA
> I keep my angst here, I preserve
> it because I need it. It keeps me
> sharp, on the edge, where I gotta
> be.

In *Heat*, Al Pacino's Det. Vincent Hanna is a cop so driven by a single-minded obsession with stalking his prey, he scarcely admits to the desolate absence of communication with his wife Justine.

>   JUSTINE HANNA
>   You don't live with me, you live
>   among the remnants of dead people.
>   You sift through the detritus, you
>   read the terrain, you search for
>   signs of passing, for the scent of
>   your prey... That's the only thing
>   you're committed to. The rest is
>   the mess you leave as you pass
>   through.

The choice is there for him to make, but Hanna is so habit-
uated to life beyond the emotional pale that he cannot come
home from the chase.

✓ **IS WILLING TO DIE FOR A CAUSE.** Of all film genres, Action-
Adventure is unique in its single most distinctive feature
— the readiness of the protagonist to face death. No well-
drawn character, any more than any normal human being, is
eager to die in meaningless self-sacrifice. However, given
the decisive confrontation between good and evil, the Action-
Adventure protagonist is prepared to make the ultimate gift
of life in order to defend an abstract ideal. Of course, even
the character may not recognize the action as an altruistic
sacrifice. Almost certainly the potential for death occurs in
the defense of more tangible grounds. A soldier may charge
a machine gun nest in order to save his platoon from
extermination. A cop may risk disarming a live bomb to
protect the lives of innocent bystanders. A gunfighter may
hang back to guard the pass so his comrades can escape. All
of these actions have observable, pragmatic motivations, but

underlying the down-to-earth is the sure and certain knowledge that thankless, eternal oblivion awaits. The moral impulse, whether articulated or not, is the larger social value represented by the tactical objective. There is much more than mere freedom at stake when the allied prisoners stage their ingenious breakout in *The Great Escape*, and more than just liberation when Luke Skywalker dive-bombs the Death Star in *Star Wars*. And in *The African Queen*, when Charlie (Humphrey Bogart) and Rose (Katherine Hepburn) undertake to blow up a German gunboat in Africa at the start of World War I, they will almost certainly die. Their action, even if successful, will hardly influence the war in the least, but it will be a slight blow for "God, King, and Country," to uphold the ideals of democracy.

RIDE IT LIKE YOU OWN IT!

The Action-Adventure protagonist is larger-than-life and twice as grand, a character who knows that action is required to prevent evil from devastating society. There is *no one else* who is able to tackle the job, and no one else who is willing to take the necessary risks for the salvation of a social order that may actually seem almost hostile to the protagonist. Nevertheless, that culture, however frail, embodies principles that the protagonist firmly holds to be absolute truth, and that are worth giving up life itself to defend. It is a high moral calling, worthy of only the most excellent of our species — what we ourselves would be if only we could.

"YOU WANT ME, YOU'RE GOING TO HAVE TO COME AND GET ME!"

— *LITTLE CAESAR*

How cheerfully he seems to grin,
How neatly spread his claws,
And welcome little fishes in
With gently smiling jaws!

— Lewis Carroll, *Alice's Adventures in Wonderland*

But the Action-Adventure antagonist is just as powerfully motivated as the protagonist, is equally willing to risk death, and is also a larger-than-life figure — who is *morally different*. Thus the hero is obliged not only to act, but to question the motives for doing so. These powerful opposing forces inevitably must slam together in a Showdown battle for truth. For that battle to be credible, and satisfying for the audience, the conflict must be between the Action-Adventure protagonist and an opponent who is worthy of the struggle, that is, one who is as fully dimensional as the protagonist.

THE ACTION-ADVENTURE ANTAGONIST:

✓ **IS A PERSONIFIED INDIVIDUAL.** Though the overriding opposition may be broadly defined, such as the Nazi war machine, an Action-Adventure protagonist must have a face to attach to the evil so that when the final Showdown comes, there is someone to actually fight against. It is difficult for the audience to feel triumph, even by winning a decisive battle, if they do not have the satisfaction of having eliminated a key figure in the making of the evil. It is possible that the predominant antagonist may not be the functional antagonist in the film, as neither the Emperor in *Star Wars* nor Adolph Hitler in World War II movies is normally the hand-to-hand enemy, but in these cases there must be a Darth Vader or a stand-in for *Der Fuhrer* so that the protagonist, and the plot, have someone specific to battle.

✓ **IS A FULLY DIMENSIONAL CHARACTER.** Altogether too often, the antagonist in Action-Adventure films is unworthy of the protagonist's energies, nothing more than a drooling psychopath whose motivation for evil is simply *to be evil.* John Lithgow's Eric Qualen in *Cliffhanger* sneers far beyond any obligatory scenery chewing, but, then, his character is trapped in a plot of remarkable silliness where there is very little for him to do but twitch with bizarre idiosyncrasies and titter maniacally. In contrast, the real antagonist in *The Silence of the Lambs* is Jame "Buffalo Bill" Gumb. He is the evil that must be stopped, but because the character cannot engage in a direct confrontation with the protagonist without destroying the element of suspense, the author of the novel, Thomas Harris, shrewdly substitutes the beguiling Dr. Hannibal Lecter as the disconcerting *presence* of Jame Gumb. In this way, the antagonist becomes a fully-realized character even though there is comparatively little screen time allotted to him. In *Enemy at the Gates*, Ed Harris' Major Konig is, in fact, a far more dimensional, interesting, and worthwhile character than the nominal protagonist Vasilli Zaitsev. We are given insights into Konig's motivations, his doubts, and, above all, his profound sense of duty that are completely absent from the main character. Partly as a consequence of this lopsided character exposition, the story bogs down in stagnant repetition until we are grateful for the antagonist's scenes because we know that he, at least, will make something happen.

✓ **IS NOT STUPID.** The one-room apartment suddenly erupts in automatic gunfire. The front door splinters off its hinges as the antagonist kicks his way inside, unleashing an unholy hail of lead on the defenseless room. Nothing inanimate or vertebrate could withstand such an angry barrage. The very walls burn with riddled holes. The antagonist blasts in the bathroom door. The choking haze of pulverized tile fills the tiny space. The antagonist edges forward to push the smoldering shower curtain away from the porcelain tub — where the girl hiding inside surges upward to stab him to death. This antagonist is a nincompoop of the highest order, a lifeless game board piece, created to do the writer's bidding.

An Action-Adventure antagonist, in all likelihood, is brighter, better educated, and much better prepared than the protagonist. The antagonist is a strategist, who has made careful, foolproof plans to reach a specific goal. The Action-Adventure protagonist is thrust into the antagonist's Narrative Trajectory, like it or not, at a high-pressure point when the antagonist's objective is already in sight. Det. John McClane has no intention of being caught in a building by a gang of super-crooks. Tom Hanks' Capt. John Miller certainly never plans to be sent into enemy territory in search of Pvt. Ryan. The protagonist, therefore, begins the drama at a disadvantage, an underdog who must continually play catch-up to the antagonist's superior tactics and resources. Yet, it is only because of the protagonist's interjection that the antagonist is diverted from the goal and, in due course, must face down the protagonist, who will seek to block evil's path to success.

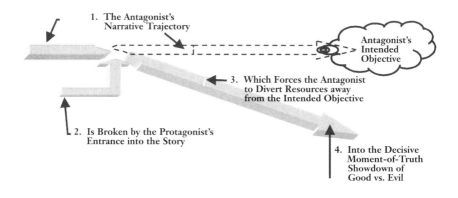

1. The Antagonist's Narrative Trajectory

Antagonist's Intended Objective

3. Which Forces the Antagonist to Divert Resources away from the Intended Objective

2. Is Broken by the Protagonist's Entrance into the Story

4. Into the Decisive Moment-of-Truth Showdown of Good vs. Evil

✓ **FORCES THE PROTAGONIST TO ACT.** The antagonist is always bigger, meaner, and has more resources than the protagonist. If not, then the protagonist would walk over the opposition. There would be no dramatic conflict and therefore no story. Just as important, the antagonist needs to be more powerful than the surrounding sycophants. Beware the *one-legged albino dwarf*! It is often easy, and fun, for screenwriters to create secondary and tertiary villains who have intriguing aberrations of body, or one-of-a-kind skills like Odd Job in *Goldfinger*. The treachery of these *one-legged albino dwarfs* is that they become absorbing in and of themselves, to the damnation of the story. If the eight-foot, red-headed nun assassin could carry a story by herself, then we should be watching *that* movie. Otherwise, the chief antagonist must be the baddest of the bunch, or the barrel of flying monkeys will steal the story's thunder. Moreover, the protagonist must necessarily fight through the subordinate antagonists to get to the final confrontation with the big guy. If that antagonist is so flawed in resolve, or so incapable of individually pursuing the goal, then the protagonist will easily have the upper hand and, therefore, cannot be tested sufficiently to satisfy the audience. By the time John McClane confronts Alan Rickman's brilliant portrayal of Hans Gruber in *Die Hard*, we have witnessed the absolute ruthlessness and remarkable cunning of this character in operation. No matter how tough McClane may be, he is in way over his head against Gruber, a gifted master of psychopathology whose sole weakness is his own ego.

✓ HAS A MORALLY DIFFERENT POINT OF VIEW. In the first instance, the antagonist's goal must be important enough to threaten the society that the protagonist is duty-bound to defend. That society may not directly encompass something as large as all of Western civilization, but it is a microcosm of the values shared by "our" side. But not only is the antagonist's goal a direct threat to society, it is a direct benefit to the antagonist, and is consistent with the antagonist's view of the world. In other words, the antagonist commits actions that, from his point of view, *are* morally justifiable. In fact, if we in the audience shared a society with the antagonist, that character would be our *protagonist*. For many people in Germany, for example, as well as for a significant population of Europe outside the Third Reich, the Nazi philosophy was a righteous undertaking. A well-drawn Nazi antagonist, then, believes strongly that the cause is just and worth sacrificing life to achieve. It is this Commitment to values that are morally different that makes a drama worthwhile. In the often repeated Western plot of the ranchers against the farmers, we in the audience are most often set to sympathize with the farmers because they represent a nascent civilization of peaceful, law-abiding citizens. However, there is a valid point of view from the other side, most often represented as the rapacious ranchers who will stop at nothing to destroy the fragile roots of an agrarian civilization. The fact is that the ranchers have an equally valid case for the use of the land; so a good Action-Adventure story could be constructed that portrays the farmers as trespassers on God's own open prairies.

The characters of Action-Adventure drama, then, are more than mere humans, even if their origins are mundane and their impulses are the most prosaic of human emotions — anger, fear, outrage, or cowardice itself. But these characters rise above their foundation, noble or commonplace, to do something on behalf of an idea, code, society, or value that is challenged by an equally motivated antagonist who is *morally different*. These opposing champions, each willing to die for a point of view, face each other in a battle for truth.

Scribble Exercise:

❏ Who was the most malicious, intractable person you have ever come into conflict with when you were a child? What issue or action set the two of you directly on opposite sides of each other? How was the confrontation settled? By words? By actions? By avoidance?

❏ Who was the most malicious, intractable person you have ever come into conflict with as an adult? What issue or action set the two of you directly on opposite sides of each other? How was the confrontation settled? By words? By actions? By avoidance?

❏ Outline the major events that escalated the conflict *from your opponent's point of view.* What values did your opponent hold? Why was your opponent willing to engage in a battle with you for the sake of those values?

❏ To what extent did each of you represent and fight for the values of a community, no matter how small that group of people?

CHAPTER EIGHT

THE ADVENTURE OF ACTION-ADVENTURE

FILM IS NOT A VISUAL MEDIUM.

Film is not a *visual* medium. It is no more a visual medium because it includes pictures than dance is an auditory medium because it includes music. Film is a *sensual* medium. It stimulates more than just our visual and auditory senses because, through these, we are made to feel and taste and even smell the world created on the screen. The scenes of the Normandy Invasion in Steven Spielberg's *Saving Private Ryan* are some of the most magnificently *sensual* experiences ever shown in a theater. The use of all the cinematic resources causes a visceral reaction in the audience that strikes much more deeply than the distress of even the most graphic Horror films, or the luscious aphrodisiac of the finest love scenes. *Saving Private Ryan* brings an audience as close to the experience of taking a beachhead as they are ever going to get without risking actual death.

"GIVE TO AIRY NOTHING A LOCAL HABITATION AND A NAME."

— WILLIAM SHAKESPEARE, *A MIDSUMMER NIGHT'S DREAM*

What *Saving Private Ryan* and other great Action-Adventure films accomplish is the creation of a romantic world. Now, it may seem odd to identify a film this gut-wrenchingly intense as *romantic*, but for the sake of investigating Action-Adventure, romantic is a usefully encompassing term. *Romance* is "such stuff as dreams are made of."[9] Our cinematic dreams are manufactured by many, many people working together to achieve an effect. Surely the film is the product of a director, but also a cinematographer, an art director, actors, set decorators, sound mixers, and all the other craftspeople who contribute to the world of the film. But long before any of these can work their magic, Romance is in the mind's eye of the screenwriter who creates mythic proportions from snatches of everyday reality, and lures our wits into a Cosmos of Credibility.

THE COSMOS OF CREDIBILITY

When an audience enters the theater, it does so with what is called the *willing suspension of disbelief*. The moviegoers know that what they are about to see is not *real*. In fact, they come to the movie precisely because they want to experience something

---

[9] *The Tempest*, William Shakespeare.

that makes more sense than the *real* world. Moreover, they expect the world of the movie to be not only sharper and more comprehensible than the everyday world they live in, but to provide them with a paradigm for the way the real world ought to be or could be. This is especially true of Action-Adventure. Remember one of the defining qualities of Action-Adventure as outlined in Chapter Three:

✓ **A ROMANTIC EXPLOIT** that transports us to a world removed from our daily existence, where the stakes are life and death, and the characters act with an intensity and nobility that we would possess if only we could.

Yet, for the screenwriter there an intrinsic dilemma that exists in shaping a Cosmos of Credibility. Cinematic reality is a very intensified facsimile of the everyday sights and sounds outside the theater. However, the viewing experience for the audience is one of largely passive acceptance of a reality that the imaginers place on the screen, which is unlike the experience of novels and short stories, for example, where anything is possible because readers sketch the suggestions of character or location in their minds. So, while film can transport us to a fantasy realm or, in the case of Action-Adventure, a Romantic one, when we are placed inside that cinematic reality it takes on an aesthetically tangible form. There is a basic aesthetic difference in how our senses adjust to the dichotomy between imagination and reality. The movie is real to our perceptions, and therefore must be judged by our experience of the real world we live in; but at the same time, it is a not-real world that is bound by the rules of a limited universe that has been created solely for one unique story.

What are the rules? Remember that the screenwriter has com-pressed time and selected the events of the drama. That means the screenwriter has already established the rules by setting up a particular, artificial context, and now must be very skillful in maintaining the Cosmos of Credibility generated by those boundaries. The paradox is that while the audience members want to have the experience of the hyper-reality, they are continually asking questions based on their sense of how the authentic outside-the-doors reality works. In other words, the screenwriter has to sell the hyper-reality to the moviegoers in such a way that they never have the opportunity to ask, *But why don't the characters just...?* If the audience ever asks the *But why don't they just...?* question without receiving a context-appropriate answer, the implicit contract of trust in the filmmakers is broken. Thus, the Cosmos of Credibility is violated, and the audience will never be able to completely reenter the special world of the movie.

ANY SIMILARITY TO HISTORICAL CHARACTERS, LIVING OR DEAD IS PURELY ACCIDENTAL. IF THE STORY IS NOT THE WAY IT WAS — THEN IT'S THE WAY IT SHOULD HAVE BEEN, AND FURTHERMORE THE AUTHOR DOES NOT GIVE A PLUG DAMN.

— JOHN MILIUS, *THE LIFE AND TIMES OF JUDGE ROY BEAN*

At the end of the day, film is a collaborative medium, and the actual Cosmos of Credibility varies from film to film, so this is an exceptionally elusive concept to define. Getting a fix on its components is like taking a still photograph of the heavens. No matter what angle we use, huge areas will be unseen because we ourselves are inside the picture, and the instant the shutter is released, the motionless image is already invalid in a speeding, spiraling universe. Nevertheless, we can examine some broad, representative quadrants of stars and try to extrapolate a sense of the whole cosmos from its parts.

THE ACTION-ADVENTURE
COSMOS OF CREDIBILITY

- **NARRATIVE TRAJECTORY** — Action-Adventure stories progress from the compression of a state of siege in which the protagonist and society are under the control of the antagonist or, in some cases, where the protagonist must penetrate the fortress of the antagonist to prohibit controlling power. Ordinarily, the crushing pressure of the siege forces the protagonist to crack the barriers in an all-out attack that takes the form of a chase ending in the culminating battle of good vs. evil. There is a clear distinction between those on the "inside" and those on the "outside" of the siege. To lose the siege is to lose possession of the culture. The protagonist fights not just for a momentary triumph, but for the very existence of the threatened society.

- **BOUNDED WORLD** — Action-Adventure occurs in a Romantic, larger-than-life world, an environment exaggerated beyond our familiar existence, where heroic action is possible even in the most ordinary circumstances. Places and artifacts are magnified, and often used in ways unimaginable in the reality of the everyday. Nevertheless, the world of Action-Adventure is governed by the physical laws of reality (unless those laws have been specifically altered within the context of the film). Available space tends to open outward from the initial confinement of the siege to the chase and final battle.

- **PLAUSIBLE MOMENT** — The Action-Adventure antagonist's plan is already in motion. The threat to society is imminent. The protagonist must act immediately, even without sufficient time to plan. Available time shrinks as the antagonist nears the objective, thereby increasing pressure on the protagonist to take risks.

- **CHARACTER ETHOS** — Action-Adventure dramas are an expression of high moral order. At the moment of truth, a protagonist infused with a code of values defends a weakened society against an equally motivated antagonist who is made of morally different stuff. It is a Showdown of good against evil between characters who are larger than life and twice as grand. They are what we ourselves would be if only we could.

"NO MAN IN THE WRONG CAN STAND UP AGAINST A FELLOW
THAT'S IN THE RIGHT AND KEEPS ON A-COMIN'."

— CAPT. LEANDER H. MCNELLY, TEXAS RANGERS

The foundation of Action-Adventure is physical action. An Action-Adventure protagonist enters the drama at a point where, for one reason or another, all attempts at negotiation, charm, tactics, and reconciliation have either already failed or are clearly of no use against an antagonist who is committed to a plan of destruction or dominance. There are no other options available except physical force.

If, in dramatic terms, the antagonist is thoroughly committed to achieving an objective that is antithetical to the values of the protagonist, and if that antagonist is bigger, meaner, stronger, and more resourceful than the protagonist (and the represented society), *and* if the introduction of the protagonist causes the antagonist to be diverted from the intended course of action, then the antagonist forces the protagonist to act in a physically decisive manner. In other words, both protagonist and antagonist *will commit violence* against each other.

The debate over the societal effect of violence in the media is beyond the scope of this book, but because Action-Adventure drama in all its forms is certainly the most physically aggressive of styles on the Genre Continuum, violence is a Cosmos-of-Credibility ingredient that cannot be ignored.

"IN ITALY FOR THIRTY YEARS UNDER THE BORGIAS THEY HAD WARFARE, TERROR, MURDER, BLOODSHED, BUT THEY PRODUCED MICHELANGELO, LEONARDO DA VINCI, AND THE RENAISSANCE. IN SWITZERLAND THEY HAD BROTHERLY LOVE, 500 YEARS OF DEMOCRACY AND PEACE. AND WHAT DID THEY PRODUCE? THE CUCKOO CLOCK."

— ORSON WELLES, AS HARRY LIME IN *THE THIRD MAN*

The actual definition of what constitutes violence has become more of a political dispute than a linguistic one; partly for that reason, the passionate arguments on all sides of the issue either ignore or grossly distort the only real significance of the term that the concept should have for screenwriters. Like pornography, art, and beauty, violence seems to be in the eye of the beholder. For the ancient Greeks, dramatic violence was considered a spiritual necessity that performed a cleansing of the soul called *catharsis*. The Greeks regularly flocked into the amphitheatres to experience the conniving murders in the adulterous House of Agamemnon, and the humiliation of Oedipus ripping his own eyes from their sockets. Of course, most of the Greek violence occurred off-stage. It was enough for the refinement of Attic culture to be aware of such tortures. Not so for the Romans. Slaughter and suffering were mother's milk for the attendees at the Coliseum. The Victorians were convinced that they could control violence through logic and science as surely as they had conquered the planet. Sherlock Holmes is the epitome of the Victorian mind, pure intellect mastering the atavistic brute.

Throughout the ages, cultures have employed the existence of human violence as barometer of community values, and it will be a very long time indeed before historians get a clear fix on the contribution film violence has made to the shape of Western civilization.

VIOLENCE VS. CONSEQUENCE

Nevertheless, for the sake of Action-Adventure films, violence has to be judged first within the framework of the Narrative Trajectory, that is, the driving forward of the cause-and-effect plot; and, second, within the Cosmos of Credibility, i.e., how it fits the style and content of the storytelling. If we define violence broadly as the exertion of physical force so as to injure another living being into incapacitation, then the term can cover just about anything — from horrific death on the beach at Normandy, to Wile E. Coyote flattened by a ten-ton safe.

This definition, however linguistically useful, does not take into account the narrative function of the physical violence. The fact is that violence, no less than car chases and love scenes, is dramatically static. Although there may be something happening on the screen, there is *nothing happening* to the story. It is not until the *result* of the violence becomes apparent that the Narrative Trajectory moves forward. A character makes a decision to act. That decision involves the use of physical force. The physical force is directed at another character with the intent of removing the impediment that character presents. There is a fight, shoot-out, ambush, sabotage, or some other violent action.

So far, absolutely nothing has happened. The violent action can go on for five seconds or five hours, and the audience members will know nothing more about the narrative than they did when the character decided to undertake the action. Not until the violent action is finished does the plot advance. Did the character win? Lose? Win what? Lose what? At what cost? These are the questions that must now be answered in order for the story to move forward. Unfortunately, all too often screenwriters ignore this most basic precept and indulge in gratuitous, meaningless, even sadistic acts of violence that produce no dramatic results. It is precisely this negligent writing that invites the social criticism of films as excessively violent. It is not the acts of violence themselves that should be disparaged, or even the quantity of those acts — but whether or not those violent acts have direct and observable consequences.

"TIMES ARE BAD. CHILDREN NO LONGER OBEY THEIR PARENTS, AND EVERYONE IS WRITING A BOOK."

— MARCUS TULLIUS CICERO, 106–43 B.C.

Perhaps more important for Action-Adventure, the loose definition of violence as physical force ignores exactly the latitude of film-maker intent and audience effect suggested by the wide range of films included in the genre. Clearly, although all Action-Adventure films contain the same basic elements of context, the emphasis changes with the particular style in which the story is told. All films require the willing suspension of disbelief from the audience, but in some cases the audience is willing to grant the filmmakers far more license because the screenwriter has set up the rules of a context that the audience recognizes is not intended to be real in any representational sense. Certainly, for example, no cartoon character is expected to suffer permanent harm from the slings and arrows of animated film, as expressed so delightfully in *Who Framed Roger Rabbit?*, but an arrow sunk into the chest of a character in *Braveheart* is delivered under entirely different Cosmos-of-Credibility rules.

In this way, we can actually use violence as a measuring rod to help determine the Cosmos of Credibility of the many styles of film storytelling that fall within the larger category of Action-Adventure. How does the audience know how to react to a particular style of film? Do they know that when Indiana Jones kills someone it isn't "for real," but that when Det. John McClane performs the same action it is — except that it is not so authentic when compared to, for instance, the deaths in *Bonnie and Clyde* or *Saving Private Ryan*? If the filmmakers have carefully constructed their Cosmos of Credibility, the audience will have no difficulty distinguishing what is *real* death from various grades of not-death.

In other words, if we use *perceived pain or grief* felt by the audience as the compass reading, then the audience's identification with the veracity of the cinema experience increases in a direct relationship. A character in an Indiana Jones movie can be sliced into lunch meat by a whirling airplane propeller, and our response is an amused groan, but a character can be severed in half by an artillery blast on the Normandy beachhead in *Saving Private Ryan*, and we will reflexively look away in genuine horror. We may know rationally that the actor did not die, but the *perceived reality* set up by the Cosmos of Credibility is such that our sensation of genuine pain and death is very palpable indeed.

CONTEXT LATITUDE — THE EXTENT OF PAIN

INTENSIFICATION OF AUDIENCE-PERCEIVED PAIN OR GRIEF

FANTASTIC	EXTRAVAGANT	LEGENDARY	EXPLICIT
Time Bandits	*Indiana Jones*	*Lawrence of Arabia*	*Saving Private Ryan*
Starship Troopers	*Superman*	*Ben-Hur*	*The Bridge on the River Kwai*
The X-Men	*Con Air*	*The Man Who Would Be King*	*Battleground*
Batman	*Rumble in the Bronx*	*The Wind and the Lion*	*Ride with the Devil*
Stargate	*Star Wars*	*The Great Escape*	*Bonnie and Clyde*
	Independence Day	*Gladiator*	
	Lethal Weapon	*The African Queen*	
	Die Hard	*Braveheart*	
		Viva Zapata!	
		Spartacus	

"HOW YOU DO ANYTHING IS HOW YOU DO EVERYTHING."

— ZEN PROVERB

We are a narrative species. We know our place in the universe and shape nearly every human endeavor by telling stories about ourselves. Whether or not we get the stories right may be the test of whether or not our culture endures. We depend on stories about the past to predict the failures and successes of the future, and those stories that prove to be true become the myths by which we live. They remind us over and over again of the values shared by our culture. Our ancestors died to protect those myths, and we bond daily in our society through their retelling. They are more than mere entertainment. The myths contain our moral obligation, our code of honor, and the expression of our willingness to die for values that have been passed to us through the generations.

More than any other film genre, Action-Adventure balances each of us at the moment of truth. We stand alone, face to face with death in the dusty street. It squints unblinking into our hearts to draw from us the same plea asked by James Ryan in *Saving Private Ryan* as he stands beside the grave of Capt. John Miller:

"Tell me I'm a good man."

163

ACTION-ADVENTURE: THE EUROPEAN PERSPECTIVE

BY
AMUND LIE

The Action-Adventure film, as Neill explores the genre in the foregoing chapters, is something to which most European audiences and filmmakers mainly have no intellectual or expe- riential connection. Not only are our production budgets very much smaller, but our familiarity with the vocabulary of action is severely limited. To be sure we recognize action when we see it on screen, but for most of us, the events are very distant from our lives. In the European mind, the action in an American film is synonymous with handling a gun or driving a car — common, everyday objects in America, but exotic tools in post-war Europe. In most countries people needed special permits just to buy a car, even up until the mid-sixties. No wonder that for Europeans the focus of American action movies has been perceived, in a social sense, to be excessive, and a perversion of the filmic art.

"You have to develop your characters more. You must give them more depth and personality." European scriptwriters are commonly confronted with this phrase uttered by a film-financing executive employed at a government-run film funding office in a typical Western European country. In translation this means that you must never write anything that could be mistaken for one of those pointless American-type action movies. The action of your protagonist just standing alone in an open field looking pensive, or taking on the French legal system in order to regain a lost child is of less importance than the requirement that your script say something meaningful. The small amount of money that is available for film funding from government resources must always be spent on the right kind of film — one that will spearhead a country's cultural values against the flood of Americanized pop culture that threatens to overtake the very foundations of national identity. So, money goes to whichever film fits a set of unwritten rules about what is politically and socially defined as important. It is not even expected that such a film make a profit. This is about culture and national identity, not capital. What is at stake is that we are buying ourselves a cultural alibi for excluding the so-called American style of filmmaking.

For many of today's European filmmakers who developed their imagery through watching Western movies on Sunday afternoons in the fifties and sixties, *action* somehow became the same as *adventure* — but not vice versa. No one in Europe even uses the word adventure in the sense of an expressive story when they speak of American movies. As a result, many European filmmakers believe that in order to make an American-style movie, you have only to create lots of action on the screen, as the Chinese do quite blatantly in their own choreographed way. The action then becomes the story by itself without any attempt to provide motivation.

Of course, the notion of the solitary adventurer is also somewhat remote in Europe. It's not that Europeans find the lone rebel unbelievable so much as oddly out of place. Why stand up for yourself when it makes no difference anyway? There's no one to support you if you win. A single person simply cannot make a difference in Europe. The solution to a problem must be legislative to have any effect. So, to engage in an adventure alone on behalf of someone else is not something we do because it wouldn't make any sense.

And here we are back to the difference between American and European filmmaking. Because we think that American films are only about action and not the noble cause of heroic deeds, we also judge the films to be of a lesser value. So, when we make our European movies, it is the deeds and not the action that are emphasized, simply because the action is perceived to have no value at all.

Is the European director not capable of making an Action-Adventure? A quick look at Hollywood history indicates that they definitely can. European directors have for many years had a major influence on the American film industry. Some of the very best, arguably the best, American films have had European directors. Could there be any clearer indicator that the European film production environment does not treat its own children right?

I believe the European perception of American movies is a misunderstanding more than anything else, a misunderstanding that action movies are only about doing something spectacular and not about the pursuit of a higher cause.

Yet the Action-Adventure genre constitutes so much more that in fact, it could encompass a major part of the films that have been made in more than one hundred years of filmmaking. Action-Adventure is the ultimate story, the basis of storytelling yesterday, today, and tomorrow. Perhaps this style of storytelling has simply been forgotten in Europe, muddled up in a relentless pursuit of sociological importance. Perhaps we need to gather around the campfire once again and get back to those eternal tales of knights and maidens, be it in shining armor or tin-foil space suits.

We must take back this fundamental form of storytelling, return to our roots, so to speak. The Action-Adventure story does not in itself originate in Hollywood, and does not belong to any particular country. In this book, Neill points out that the fundamental Action-Adventure leaves plenty of room for personal interpretation. It is a universal genre that is about telling a good story. And that is, perhaps, the major impact of this book — that there is a whole lot more to the genre than one might have thought in the first place. It has led me to believe that making the *European* Action-Adventure is quite possible after all.

Amund Lie is a Norwegian-born director, scriptwriter and editor who divides his time between running Hook Digital, his special effects company in London, England, and developing feature-film projects from his current home in Vancouver, Canada.

EPILOGUE

September 11, 2001

This book goes to press in the aftermath of the terrorist attack on the World Trade Center in New York. It is too soon to know what consequences this enormity will have for American society, much less for the American movie industry.

The terrorists who perpetrated the atrocity targeted their assault at what they perceived to be American monuments to world dominion. Prior to their actions, it is doubtful that many Americans beyond the confines of New York City would have identified the World Trade Center as an icon of our country, but the terrorists have now succeeded in creating a "Remember the Alamo" war cry that resonates for every citizen.

That they mistook their symbols for ours, reveals their blind misconception of the American character — a moral fiber that is readily on display for all to see in the cowboys and cops of our Action-Adventure films.

Amidst the rubble at Ground Zero are thousands of heroes, New York Police and Fire department personnel, iron workers, plumbers, carpenters, and ordinary citizen volunteers who did not ask to be champions of the American spirit, but who have become our emblem of collective defiance.

The extraordinary passengers on United Flight 93 did not board the airplane expecting to become heroes. Nevertheless, when fate intervened, they stood up and did the right thing because it was the right thing to do. The insignia of their selfless actions will be knit into the fabric of the cultural narrative by American storytellers for many years to come.

Even in circumstances of much less renown, everyday Americans have accepted the responsibility of their legendary birthright. As the dust settled around the destroyed financial center, the employees of Sun Microsystems took it upon themselves without any company authorization to put together servers and work stations, then personally deliver the equipment to their clients so that the crucial economic network could get up and running again.

The terrorists who attack buildings fail to grasp that our icons are not made in stone, but in celluloid. The veins of every American are suffused with the mythic blood of Will Kane. Soon these idolaters will come to know the fury of a people who, by God, do what has to be done.

NDH
September, 2001

GLOSSARY

A few terms used in *Screenwriting 101: The Essential Craft of Feature Film Writing* have been refined or expanded in *Writing the Action-Adventure Film*. In all likelihood, more terms will be further refined in the upcoming *Writing the Thriller Film* in order to characterize how equivalent structural functions acquire different qualities in each of the genres.

Writing the Action-Adventure Film	*Screenwriting 101*	Use
Bounded World	physical world	The idiosyncrasies of the special, limited physical world in which the story takes place.
Briefing	backstory	Certain events occurred in the past that established the conditions of the current story. Because the plots of Action-Adventure stories are ordinarily not very complicated, there is generally very little Briefing required to get started.
Comedic Drama	comedy	Adults act like children when confronted by a basic misunderstanding that is never dealt with rationally.

Commitment	obsession	The antagonist drives the pro-tagonist into a compulsion to support a moral principle. If the protagonist fails to defend society's values, the society itself will fall victim to the antagonist.
Debriefing	self-realization	The protagonist is defeated; left alone with the skeleton of fear and doubt, to confront death and answer the demand of deed over word.
Impossible Mission	goal	The urgency of the initial contact focuses the main character on a specific target: an Impossible Mission to destroy an enemy fortification, defend a position against superior numbers, or capture an object or territory.
Initial Contact	inciting incident	The protagonist must person-ally take immediate, decisive action to protect society from the menace presented by the antagonist.
Join-up	new beginnings	The protagonist defeats the antagonist, securing society's values and a place in that society.

Metaphysical Defiance	metaphysical struggle	The protagonist risks his or her immortal soul by challenging the authority of a self-indulgent Almighty.
Narrative Trajectory	dramatic emphasis	The inherent sense of a story's dramatic hook rising through anticipation to the height of complication, and the promise of a final, satisfying resolution.
Pivotal Conflict	interpersonal conflict	Characters are forced to restore a relationship by resolving emotional wounds.
Plausible Moment	time	The apparent elapsed time that the audience senses of how long it takes for the story to unfold, as well as the encompassing era of the story.
Private Anguish	intrapersonal anguish	Characters' self-revelation through the expiation of guilt or imagined guilt.
Reconnoiter	preparation	The protagonist devises a strategy for achieving the impossible mission, and assembles resources, equipment, and professional team members.

Showdown	battle	Compromise between the main character and the antagonist is impossible. They must fight in a moment of truth to determine the survival not of people, but of a value.
Skeleton Pack	internal need	No matter how courageous, the protagonist always carries a skeleton backpack into combat, a set of values that has never been tested under fire, but now will be called into question through conflict with the antagonist.
Target Acquisition	antagonist	Identification of an antagonist who threatens the society with more power, greater resources, and a morally different stance than the protagonist.

REFERENCED FILMS

FILM TITLE	YEAR	SCREENWRITER(S)	DIRECTOR(S)
African Queen, The	1951	James Agee from the C. S. Forester novel	John Huston
Alamo, The	1960	James Edward Grant	John Wayne
Alien	1979	Dan O'Bannon from a story by Dan O'Bannon and Ronald Shusett (David Giler & Walter Hill, uncredited)	Ridley Scott
Apocalypse Now	1979	John Milius and Francis Ford Coppola from the Joseph Conrad novel, *Heart of Darkness*	Francis Ford Coppola
Armageddon	1998	Jonathan Hensleigh and J.J. Abrams; adaptation by Tony Gilroy and Shane Salerno from a story by Robert Roy Pool and Johnathan Hensleigh	Michael Bay
Battle of the Bulge	1965	Bernard Gordon, John Melson, Milton Sperling	Ken Annakin
Battleground	1949	Robert Pirosh	William Wellman
Ben-Hur	1959	Karl Tunberg from the Lew Wallace novel (Maxwell Anderson and Christopher Fry and Gore Vidal, uncredited)	William Wyler
Bone Collector, The	1999	Jeremy Iacone from the Jeffery Deaver novel	Philip Noyce
Bonnie and Clyde	1967	Robert Benton & David Newman (Robert Towne, uncredited)	Arthur Penn
Bravados, The	1958	Philip Yordan from the Frank O'Rourke novel	Henry King
Braveheart	1995	Randall Wallace	Mel Gibson
Bridges at Toko-Ri	1954	Valentine Davis from the novel by James Michener	Mark Robson
Butch Cassidy and the Sundance Kid	1969	William Goldman	George Roy Hill
Chinatown	1974	Robert Towne (Roman Polanski, uncredited)	Roman Polanski

Title	Year	Writer(s)	Director
Cliffhanger	1993	Michael France and Sylvester Stallone from a screen story by Michael France, from a premise by John Long	Renny Harlin
Copycat	1995	Ann Biderman and David Madsen	Jon Amiel
Con Air	1997	Scott Rosenberg	Simon West
Cries and Whispers	1972	Ingmar Bergman	Ingmar Bergman
Die Hard	1988	Jeb Stuart and Steven E. de Souza from the Roderick Thorp novel, *Nothing Lasts Forever*	John McTiernan
Die Hard: With a Vengeance	1995	Jonathan Hensleigh based on certain original characters by Roderick Thorp	John McTiernan
Dirty Dozen, The	1967	Nunnally Johnson and Lukas Heller from the E. M. Nathanson novel	Robert Aldrich
Dirty Harry	1971	Dean Riesner from a story by Harry Julian Fink & Rita M. Fink (John Milius, uncredited)	Don Siegel
Driving Miss Daisy	1989	Alfred Uhry from his play	Bruce Beresford
Enemy at the Gates	2001	Jean-Jacques Annaud and Alain Godard	Jean-Jacques Annaud
55 Days at Peking	1963	Bernard Gordon & Philip Yordan (Ben Barzman, uncredited)	Nicholas Ray (Andrew Marton, uncredited)
15 Minutes	2001	John Herzfeld	John Herzfeld
Full Metal Jacket	1987	Michael Herr & Stanley Kubrick from the Gustav Hasford novel, *The Short Timers*	Stanley Kubrick
General, The	1927	Al Boasberg & Charlie Smith	Clyde Bruckmer & Buster Keaton
Gladiator	2000	David Franzoni and John Logan and William Nicholson from a story by David Franzoni	Ridley Scott
Godfather, The	1972	Francis Ford Coppola and Mario Puzo from the Mario Puzo novel	Francis Ford Coppola

Film	Year	Writer/Source	Director
Goldfinger	1964	Richard Maibaum & Paul Dehn from the Ian Fleming novel	Guy Hamilton
Good Will Hunting	1997	Matt Damon & Ben Affleck	Gus Van Sant
Great Escape, The	1963	James Clavell and W. R. Burnett from the Paul Brickhill novel	John Sturges
Great Northfield Minnesota Raid, The	1972	Philip Kaufman	Philip Kaufman
Great Train Robbery, The	1903	Edwin S. Porter	Edwin S. Porter
Gunfight at the O.K. Corral	1957	Leon Uris from an article by George Scullin	John Sturges
Guns Of Navarone, The	1961	Carl Foreman from the Alistair MacLean novel	J. Lee Thompson
Heat	1995	Michael Mann	Michael Mann
High Noon	1952	Carl Foreman from a story by John W. Cunningham	Fred Zinnemann
King Solomon's Mines	1950	Helen Deutsch from the H. Rider Haggard novel	Compton Bennet & Andrew Marton
Last Action Hero	1993	Shane Black & David Arnott from a story by Zak Penn & Adam Leff	John McTiernan
Lethal Weapon	1987	Shane Black	Richard Donner
Little Caesar	1930	Francis Edward Faragoh, Robert N. Lee, and Robert Lord from the novel by William R. Burnett (Darryl F. Zanuck, uncredited)	Mervyn LeRoy
Longest Day, The	1962	Romain Gary, James Jones, David Pursall, Cornelius Ryan, and Jack Seddon from the Cornelius Ryan novel	Ken Annakin, Andrew Marton, Gerd Oswald, and Bernhard Wicki (Darryl F. Zanuck, uncredited)
Magnificent Seven, The	1960	William Roberts (Walter Bernstein and Walter Newman, uncredited) based on an Akira Kurosawa screenplay, *Shichinin no samurai*	John Sturges
Man Who Never Was, The	1956	Nigel Balchin from the Ewen Montagu book	Ronald Neame
Man Who Shot Liberty Valance, The	1962	James Warner Bellah & Willis Goldbeck from story by Dorothy M. Johnson	John Ford

Title	Year	Screenplay	Director
Marathon Man	1976	William Goldman from his novel	John Schlesinger
Marvin's Room	1996	Scott McPherson from his play	Jerry Zacks
McCabe and Mrs. Miller	1971	Robert Altman and Brian McKay (Warren Beatty, uncredited) from the Edmund Naughton novel	Robert Altman
Moulin Rouge	2001	Baz Luhrmann & Craig Pearce	Baz Luhrmann
No Highway in the Sky	1951	R. C. Sherriff and Oscar Millard and Alec Coppel from the Neville Shute novel, *No Highway*	Henry Koster
North by Northwest	1959	Ernest Lehman	Alfred Hitchcock
Persona	1966	Ingmar Bergman	Ingmar Bergman
Poseidon Adventure, The	1972	Wendell Mayes and Stirling Silliphant from the Paul Gallico novel	Ronald Neame (Irwin Allen, uncredited)
Pretty Woman	1990	J. F. Lawton	Garry Marshall
Prince of Tides	1991	Pat Conroy and Becky Johnson from the Pat Conroy novel	Barbra Streisand
Professionals, The	1966	Richard Brooks from the Frank O'Rourke novel, *A Mule for the Marquesa*	Richard Brooks
Psycho	1960	Joseph Stefano from the Robert Bloch novel	Alfred Hitchcock
Purple Rose of Cairo, The	1985	Woody Allen	Woody Allen
Raiders of the Lost Ark	1981	Lawrence Kasdan from a story by George Lucas and Philip Kaufman	Steven Spielberg
Rain Man	1988	Ronald Bass and Barry Morrow from a story by Barry Morrow	Barry Levinson
Saving Private Ryan	1998	Robert Rodat	Steven Spielberg
Searchers, The	1956	Frank S. Nugent from the Alan LeMay novel	John Ford
Shane	1953	A. B. Guthrie from a story by Jack Schaefer (additional dialogue by Jack Sher)	George Stevens

Shichinin no samurai (Seven Samurai)	1954	Shinobu Hashimoto, Akira Kurosawa, and Hideo Oguni	Akira Kurosawa
Silence of the Lambs, The	1991	Ted Tally from the Thomas Harris novel	Jonathan Demme
Simple Plan, A	1998	Scott B. Smith from his novel	Sam Raimi
Sixth Sense, The	1999	M. Night Shyamalan	M. Night Shyamalan
Sleepy Hollow	1999	Andrew Kevin Walker from a screen story by Kevin Yagher & Andrew Kevin Walker, based on the Washington Irving story, *The Legend of Sleepy Hollow*	Tim Burton
Spartacus	1960	Dalton Trumbo (Calder Willingham and Peter Ustinov, uncredited) from the Howard Fast novel	Stanley Kubrick
Speed	1994	Graham Yost	Jan de Bont
Star Wars	1977	George Lucas	George Lucas
Sudden Impact	1983	Joseph Stinson from a story by Charles B. Pierce and Earl E. Smith	Clint Eastwood
Terminator 2: Judgment Day	1991	James Cameron & William Wisher Jr.	James Cameron
Three Days of the Condor	1975	Lorenzo Semple Jr. and David Rayfiel from the James Grady novel, *Six Days of the Condor*	Sydney Pollack
Three Kings	1999	David O. Russell from a story by John Ridley	David O. Russell
Titanic	1997	James Cameron	James Cameron
Tombstone	1993	Kevin Jarre	George Cosmatos
Towering Inferno, The	1974	Stirling Silliphant from the Richard Martin Stern novel, *The Tower*, and the Thomas N. Scortia and Frank M. Robinson novel, *The Glass Inferno*	Irwin Allen and John Guillermin
Trip to the Moon, A	1903	Georges Méliès from the Jules Verne novel	Georges Méliès
True Grit	1969	Marguerite Roberts (from the Charles Portis novel, uncredited)	Henry Hathaway

Twister	1996	Michael Crichton & Anne-Marie Martin	Jan de Bont
Usual Suspects, The	1995	Christopher McQuarrie	Bryan Singer
Viva Zapata!	1952	John Steinbeck	Elia Kazan
Wait Until Dark	1967	Robert Howard-Carrington & Jane Howard-Carrington from the Frederick Knott play	Terence Young
Who Framed Roger Rabbit?	1988	Jeffrey Price & Peter S. Seaman from the Gary K. Wolf novel, *Who Censored Roger Rabbit?*	Robert Zemeckis
Wild Bunch, The	1969	Walon Green, Sam Peckinpah, and Roy N. Sickner from a story by Walon Green and Roy N. Sickner	Sam Peckinpah
Winchester '73	1950	Robert L. Richards & Borden Chase from a story by Stuart N. Lake	Anthony Mann
Wind and the Lion, The	1975	John Milius	John Milius
Wizard of Oz, The	1939	Noel Langley and Florence Ryerson and Edgar Allan Woolf from the L. Frank Baum novel, *The Wonderful Wizard of Oz*	Victor Fleming (Richard Thorpe and King Vidor, uncredited)
Wyatt Earp	1994	Dan Gordon and Lawrence Kasdan	Lawrence Kasdan
Zulu	1964	John Prebble and Cy Endfield from an article by John Prebble	Cy Endfield

NEILL D. HICKS

After completing top-secret work for a government agency that refuses to admit his existence, Neill naturally became a screenwriter specializing in such Thriller and Action-Adventure films as Pierce Brosnan's *Don't Talk to Strangers*, and the critically acclaimed *Dead Reckoning*. At the same time, he has written the screenplays for European and Asian productions, including the Scandinavian films *The Minister of State* and *Ice Frontier*, the animated  feature of the epic Indian narrative poem the *Mahabharath*, and two simultaneous #1 box-office films in the world — Jackie Chan's *Rumble in the Bronx* and *First Strike*. He recently completed the feature story *Ghost Writer* for the Academy Award–winning Italian filmmakers of *Il Postino*. His scripts for *The Anodyne Conduct*, a chilling, near-future Political Thriller, and *The Misgiven*, a tale of romantic deceit in the cabals of the Dark Ages, are in development in Hollywood.

Neill's book, *Screenwriting 101: The Essential Craft of Feature Film Writing*, has been a worldwide success, particularly as more European and Asian filmmakers search for ways to structure their stories in a global market. His original analysis of the principles of film genre writing has created the demand that he publish a series of additional books for screenwriters on the underlying fundamentals for specific story archetypes. His consulting services are in demand on both U.S. and international productions. He probes within the structure of a screenplay to improve the Cosmos of Credibility that encourages his audience to put its trust in a story. His work is audience-focused, welding plot and character, so that he boosts the hard-line Narrative Trajectory to grab hold of what the audience instinctively cares about.

With a background in documentary as well as fiction film, Neill has also created diverse programs from WWII's *Operation Pointblank* for A&E's *Masters of War* series to the *Children's Crusade* of the 13th century for the History Channel. His work as a theatrical director has spanned productions from Gilbert and Sullivan's *The Mikado* to Shakespeare's *Taming of the Shrew*. In academia, he has been honored with the Outstanding Instructor Award at the UCLA Extension Writers' Program and has been a guest lecturer in screenwriting at Northwestern University, the University of Wisconsin, California State University, and the Canadian Television & Film Institute. He is a member of the adjunct faculty of the University of Denver, and an advisor to the Studiesenteret for Film in Oslo, Norway.

Neill is also a specialist in linguistic analysis. His company provides business seminars and private instruction in accent reduction and voice training.

SCREENWRITING 101
The Essential Craft of Feature Film Writing

Neill D. Hicks

Hicks, a successful screenwriter whose credits include *Rumble in the Bronx* and *First Strike*, brings the clarity and practical instruction familiar to his UCLA students to screenwriters everywhere. In his inimitable straight-forward style, Hicks tells the beginning screenwriter how the mechanics of Hollywood storytelling work, and how to use those elements to create a script with block-buster potential without falling into clichés. Also discussed are the practicalities of the business: securing an agent, pitching your script, and other topics essential to building a career in screenwriting.

$16.95
Order # 41RLS
ISBN: 0-941188-72-8

SCRIPT MAGIC
Subconscious Techniques to Conquer Writer's Block
Marisa D'Vari

Script Magic is a powerful antidote to writer's block that both professional and aspiring creative writers can benefit from. It's based on a deceptively simple principle: if you're not having fun creating your script, it probably isn't going to be any fun to read, either. And if it's not fun to read, how is it ever going to be sold and made into a movie that people will want to spend their money to see?

Using easy and fun techniques designed to tap into the rich creative resources of the subconscious mind, readers will learn how to revitalize their writing and improve their productivity. Create engaging characters, dialogue that jumps off the page, and screenplays that sell!

$18.95
Order # 47RLS
ISBN: 0-941188-74-4

THE WRITER'S JOURNEY
2nd Edition
Mythic Structure for Writers

Christopher Vogler

See why this book has become an international best-seller and a true classic. First published in 1992, *The Writer's Journey* explores the powerful relationship between mythology and storytelling in a clear, concise style that's made it required reading for movie executives, screenwriters, scholars, and fans of pop culture all over the world.

Both fiction and nonfiction writers will discover a set of useful myth-inspired storytelling paradigms (i.e., "The Hero's Journey") and step-by-step guidelines to plot and character development. Based on the work of Joseph Campbell, *The Writer's Journey* is a must for all writers interested in further developing their craft.

The updated and revised 2nd Edition provides new insights, observations, and film references from Vogler's ongoing work on mythology's influence on stories, movies, and man himself.

Christopher Vogler, a top Hollywood story consultant and development executive, has worked on such high-grossing feature films as The Lion King *and* The Thin Red Line *and conducts writing workshops around the globe.*

$22.95
Order # 98RLS
ISBN: 0-941188-70-1

SCREENWRITING ON THE INTERNET
Researching, Writing, and Selling Your Script on the Web

Christopher Wehner

The Internet can save you loads of money, time and effort—but only if you know how to exploit it. *Screenwriting on the Internet* is your road map to using the information superhighway to further your screenwriting career. Packed with time- and money-saving tips, this book tells you exactly where you need to go and what you need to do to get the information you want, whether you're doing research or looking to submit your screenplay to the right agent or producer.

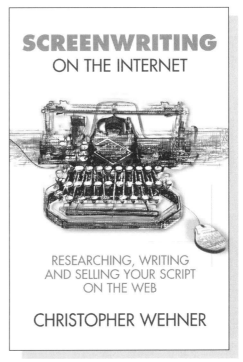

Includes step-by-step instructions on the do's and don'ts of e-mail querying, a definitive directory of over 300 industry e-mail addresses and Web sites, and much more. You'll learn how you can write your script on a beach in Maui, e-mail it to partners in London, and cash your paycheck in Hollywood!

Christopher Wehner founded The Screenwriters Utopia, which has become one of the most popular and heavily visited sites for writers on the Internet.

$16.95
Order #5RLS
ISBN: 0-941188-36-1

ORDER FORM

TO ORDER THESE PRODUCTS, PLEASE CALL **24** HOURS - **7** DAYS A WEEK
CREDIT CARD ORDERS **1-800-833-5738** OR FAX YOUR ORDER **(818) 986-3408**
OR MAIL THIS ORDER FORM TO:

MICHAEL WIESE PRODUCTIONS
11288 VENTURA BLVD., # 621
STUDIO CITY, CA 91604
E-MAIL: MWPSALES@MWP.COM
WEB SITE: WWW.MWP.COM

WRITE OR FAX FOR A FREE CATALOG

PLEASE SEND ME THE FOLLOWING BOOKS:

TITLE	ORDER NUMBER (#RLS _____)	AMOUNT
_____	_____	_____
_____	_____	_____
_____	_____	_____
_____	_____	_____
_____	_____	_____
	SHIPPING	_____
	CALIFORNIA TAX **(8.00%)**	_____
	TOTAL ENCLOSED	_____

SHIPPING:
ALL ORDERS MUST BE PREPAID, UPS GROUND SERVICE ONE ITEM - **$3.95**
EACH ADDITIONAL ITEM ADD **$2.00**
EXPRESS - **3** BUSINESS DAYS ADD **$12.00** PER ORDER
OVERSEAS
SURFACE - **$15.00** EACH ITEM   AIRMAIL - **$30.00** EACH ITEM

PLEASE MAKE CHECK OR MONEY ORDER PAYABLE TO:

MICHAEL WIESE PRODUCTIONS

(CHECKONE) ____ MASTERCARD ___VISA ____AMEX

CREDIT CARD NUMBER _____

EXPIRATION DATE _____

CARDHOLDER'S NAME _____

CARDHOLDER'S SIGNATURE _____

SHIP TO:

NAME _____

ADDRESS _____

CITY _____ STATE _____ ZIP _____

COUNTRY _____ TELEPHONE _____

ORDER ONLINE FOR THE LOWEST PRICES

24 HOURS | 1.800.833.5738 | www.mwp.com